What others say about Doug Giles

"I don't know anyone else preaching the word of God in such a refreshing, masculine manner. After all, we are talking about the Son of God. Not the Daughter of God. Not the They of God. Perhaps, like myself, God got sick of the yawping tommyrot, so he told Doug to speak up, and to use his man voice."

Jim Houck, Writer & Director

"I think Doug Giles brings a sharp, humorous, bold and captivating style to ministry that strikes a chord with young people."

Dr. R.C. Sproul

"Doug Giles is a good man, and his bambinas are fearless. His girls Hannah and Regis Giles are indefatigable. I admire the Giles clan from afar."

Dennis Miller

"Doug Giles must be some kind of a great guy if CNN wants to impugn him."

Rush Limbaugh

"Doug Giles is a substantive and funny force for traditional values."

Ann Coulter

"Doug Giles speaks the truth ... he's a societal watchdog ... a funny bastard."

Ted Nugent

What others say about Doug Giles

Doug Giles has served us up a savory dish from the Word of God, and giving us insight into God's perfect example of manhood ... Jesus! This work is real food and the perfect antidote for the thin gruel served up by much of America's mainstream church today. Let this minister to the call of God on your life, and step forward more boldly into the role of warrior, king, and priest that God has created each of us to be.

Wayne Woods, Alaska Master Guide, DD,DMin

" Wow! Halfway through the book I literally started to believe the author is nothing but a fully morphed modern incarnation of the warhammer in the hands of the raiding Crusaders, the shadow of Jesus Christ's angry fist smashing the tavern table at the misdeeds of a corrupt society wretched by its comforts. Grab your bottle and cigar and make sure the chair is sturdy! "

Radu, The Hunting Baron

"How many times have you heard someone say, "We need to be like Jesus--meek and mild." Jesus was neither. It's no accident that "Gentle Jesus, meek and mild" is from a children's prayer. Of course, there were times when Jesus was gentle with children and the infirm, but mostly He was direct, strict, and tough. He said and did things that would horrify the average churchgoer. I have many commentaries on the Gospel of Matthew but not one shows Jesus as someone determined to discredit and destroy evil wherever it is found. If Masculinity Is 'Toxic' Call Jesus Radioactive is a one-of-a-kind portrait of Jesus that will transform your thinking about Jesus."

Gary DeMar, American Vision

Dedication

This book is dedicated to all the Christian men out there who believe that just because you're a Christian it doesn't mean you have to be a tinkerpot.

Published by White Feather Press.
(www.whitefeatherpress.com)

ISBN 978-1-61808-194-0

Printed in the United States of America

Cover design by David Bugnon and mobopolis.com

If Masculinity Is 'Toxic' Call Jesus Radioactive

Written by

Doug Giles

Table of Contents

Preface

I was not raised in a Christian home. I started following Jesus at age 23 after a radical conversion experience. Having been raised by strong parents, and a father who is a former Marine and Vietnam Veteran, I could not understand the passivity of the men in the church. But I loved the church and I loved the Bible. Nine years later, in 2001, I planted and continue to pastor what is now Destiny Christian Church. From a sleepy Arizona town, I have traveled the world training and discipling thousands of pastors and leaders with my focus and passion being the underground church in Southeast Asia.

I first encountered Doug Giles through reading his articles on Clashdaily.com. Doug was a breath of fresh air! He was strong, rowdy, conservative, AND a Christian. That combination is not common in the Church today. I invited him to speak at a men's conference at Destiny. He accepted and that was the beginning of an incredible friendship and partnership in ministry. It resulted in the creation of *Warriors and Wildmen*, a podcast for men, designed to put "brains and balls on believers." Doug has also become a hero to my sons. In a world seriously lacking in godly role models, Doug has earned my respect for the example he is to my boys.

Men have lost their way in the American church today. They believe that Jesus died on the cross so they could "be nice." Men have traded in their responsibility of leading their families for a politically correct, quasi-spiritual, sissified, version of cultural Christianity. They are led by culture, instead of being the counter-cultural revolutionaries described in Romans 12:2, "Do not conform to the pattern of this world, but be transformed by the renewing of your mind." Our thinking must be dictated by the Word of God, not by the current cultural wave of weakness. That's why this book is both timely and necessary.

Concerning this book you now hold in your hand, if I could change the title, I would change it to *How To Become A Man Of God*. This could be a textbook to train men in the church how to live like Jesus! This book blew me away! Listen, I talk to Doug every week, sometimes multiple times per week. We spend 1-2 hours weekly on Skype recording the *Warriors and Wildmen* podcast. And this book still caught me off guard!

Doug is crazy! He is witty! He uses a lot of phrases that are confrontational and entertaining. But don't let that distract you from the fact that he is a serious Bible scholar and student. His insights into the masculinity of Jesus from the book of Matthew are powerful, awesome, and relevant! True biblical masculinity is needed now more than ever before! And who better to model masculinity than Jesus, the One who created us?

There are some serious and heavy truths in this book. It will challenge you, educate you, enlighten you, and inspire you. I will be using *If Masculinity Is 'Toxic' Call Jesus Radioactive* in my church to train men to become Men of God. Don't read this book if you want to continue in the status quo of cultural Christianity. It will blow that mindset to pieces! Doug takes us on a much-needed ride to biblical masculinity. Can you handle it?

Rich Witmer

Sr. Pastor and Co-host of *Warriors and Wildmen*

Chapter 1

Dear Tinkerpot Pastors: Your Jesus Is Too Nice.

"Be on the alert, stand firm in the faith, act like men, be strong."

1 Corinthians 16:13 (NASB)

2016 saw the publication of my best, best-selling book, *The Effeminization of the American Male.*

I must warn you: that book is rougher than grandma's breath. Especially if you're a slack-jawed entitled young male. Good luck with getting through that brutal tome. Oh, by the way, I suggest you put on a cup before going any further. Anyway …

Indeed, in my #1 Amazon best-seller, I took my verbal sledgehammer to the ubiquitous male tinkerpots that proliferate America's effete milieu and I did it, ironically, with schoolgirl glee.

And you know what?

It resonated with a stack of Americans and international peeps because we sold a lot of copies of that 202-page waffle-stomper.

As most of you know, I don't like to brag, and I don't like to boast, but I like hot butter on my breakfast toast: that book contains some *true* gems. Some *pure* gold.

One of the chapters I really liked/like that I thought would get minimal accolades because the book's bent was not, specifically, driven towards The Church, but more toward the unwashed masses, is my chapter, *Dear Christian: You Might Be a Wussy... But Jesus Ain't* (*Please note: that's not the *exact* title of that chapter as I'm trying to 'behave' with this book so I can have what some call a 'broader appeal'.)

I threw that very Christ-o-centric chapter into my polemic against the pusillanimous because, I believe, the Church is primarily responsible for the effeminate crap-sicle, which is postmodern America, principally because a lot of ministers are peddling a soft-focused-bearded-lady version of Jesus that has diddly squat to do with the angry young dragonslayer who kicked up dust on the mean streets of the Middle East many moons ago.

> * Here's an FYI for Pastors and Priests: don't whine about the corruption of culture and the despicable nature of most politicians when you crank out gutless puppets instead of courageous prophets.

So I threw that chapter in kind of as an 'aside'. Y'know ... just to go on record in a widely read book that I think the Church needs to be churched in regards to its rank, and I mean *rank*, self-inflicted effeminacy and how dare Christians talk smack about culture and politics when we don't have the masculine moxy the prophets, apostles and Christ Jesus himself sported in spades.

And you know what?

That quick exposition I penned on the book of Matthew, highlighting the masculine qualities of Christ in contrast to the squealy, effeminate tenor, of our current emasculated ecclesiastical emissaries has garnered more unsolicited positive feedback, especially from the 'laity', than every other chapter in my spicy read.

Can you say, 'Yahtzee?'

I think I struck a nerve.

Which brings me to this new little book about Jesus's masculinity.

Masculinity, and 'men who would be men', and 'testosterone', and 'boys just being boys', are being attacked more in this sassy society than the fudge fountain was at Rosie O'Donnell's last plus-sized pool party.

Not only is classical masculinity vilified by the mouthy misandrists but the manly qualities of Jesus are getting about as much love from the pulpit as I would if I rocked up, unannounced, to an AOC goat roast.

Ok, I'll stop with the hamfisted and childish cultural references and get to my point.

My point is, and I'll prove it in the next 30+ chapters, from the book of Matthew, that when it comes to Jesus Christ, as defined by the scripture, He's any and everything other than a Precious Moments figurine. And for *moi,* it's the sin of sins to neuter what the scripture screams about that thirty-year-old rebel from Galilee.

Doug Giles
Somewhere In Texas

Chapter 2.

Our Neutered 'Jesus' vs. The REAL Jesus

"It seems that if someone shows up preaching quite another Jesus than we preached—different spirit, different message—you put up with him quite nicely."

2 Corinthians 11:4-6 (The Message)

When the misinformed thinks of Jesus nowadays, one imagines ...

An overly ebullient, grinning hick with a curly mullet, a man bag and a quaint southern drawl, who spits out more aphorisms than Joel Osteen on crystal-meth-laced Mountain Dew.

Or The Nazarene gets painted as some rambling, Rasputin-like mystic who strings together long, illogical stories like an unshorn, Bruce Banner-inspired, Matthew McConaughey grad speech.

Either that or Jesus Christo gets pitched as some unisexual, religious, gluten-free Gucci model who might confuse us in regards to his actual gender, but he's crystal clear with his message that we should all be tolerant of the ridiculous no matter how much it offends reason.

Two things are for certain in our culture's postmodern paranormal messaging regarding Christ and Christians:

Jesus is not masculine and …

Christianity is for pansies

Indeed, our wussified culture has created for themselves a wussified, Faux Christ, who's nicer than the actual Jesus and has little to nothing to do with the rebellious, young Galilean who jettisoned evil politicians and priests and crushed *el Diablo* two-thousand-years ago.

Consequently, his followers are expected to produce gelded disciples who do not upset the world like the first century believers did.

Well, as you can imagine, Dear Reader, I'm here to blow that nonsense all to smithereens.

The real Jesus of the scripture was a very hard act to follow. I hate to disparage Jason Momoa, but the Christ of the Bible makes Jason look like Joe Exotic.

Jesus was the epitome of a man's man.

Yep, the Jesus of the scripture razed hell, drank and made wine, was a carpenter before Home Depot and power tools, fashioned a whip and turned over the book tables of the religious dandies of his day, bashed false prophets and wicked politicos and sacrificially gave up his life as a ransom for many. To make that Man into Jared Leto with Courtney Cox's coif, as far as I'm concerned, is real close to the unpardonable sin.

If you need proof that I'm not a bubble off level, then grab your journal, Dinky and sit down for this one and check out my observations of the Rowdy Christ from the Book of Matthew.

Chapter 3

Hero Savior: Matthew 1:18-21

---

18 Now the birth of Jesus Christ was as follows: when His mother Mary had been betrothed to Joseph, before they came together she was found to be with child by the Holy Spirit. 19 And Joseph her husband, being a righteous man and not wanting to disgrace her, planned to send her away secretly. 20 But when he had considered this, behold, an angel of the Lord appeared to him in a dream, saying, "Joseph, son of David, do not be afraid to take Mary as your wife; for the Child who has been conceived in her is of the Holy Spirit. 21 She will bear a Son; and you shall call His name Jesus, for He will save His people from their sins."

Matthew. 1: 18-21 (NASB)

When the average dullard reads the aforementioned they think, 'Awww. Isn't that a sweet Christmas story?' In today's parlance it would be akin to a formal, 'We're pregnant', cutesy meme on Facebook and/or Instagram.

What's missed on some, from a masculine standpoint, is

that little baby boy was born to be a Hero Savior. Yep, his mission is heroic and sacrificial. It's not a job for the squeamish 21st century hipster dandy.

This is the 'stuff' of real men. Yea, The Ultimate Man. Indeed, forget trying to replicate the macho dudes on Instagram and instead set your sights to follow Jesus' lead if you really 'wanna be a man.'

Jesus' task was a sacrificial salvaging of us sin-laden dunderheads that entailed an epic confrontation of sin in sinners, a sacrificial payment of our sin debt before a Holy God and an eternal crushing of the malevolent one, the devil.

Again, this is not a task for a guy trying to get in touch with his 'feminine side', who's afraid of confrontation and paying the ultimate price for someone else's salvation.

Please note, that the glide path The Son of God was born to take, wasn't to tell quaint, moralistic, stories in Elizabethan English.

It wasn't to be an exemplary nice boy for all the untoward ruffians to emulate.

Oh, no *senorita.*

His task was to rescue the damned from damnation.

By the way, you don't hear much about damnation anymore in churches now, do you? No one goes to hell anymore if you listen to and are to believe most ministers who drone on during their heretical eulogies at funerals.

Jesus's goal: Save His people from their sins.

Sin. There's another word that's currently being avoided and/or defined down in our ecclesiastical hovels that are taking their cue from the therapeutic community versus the *Verbum Dei.*

My former seminary professor, Dr. R.C. Sproul, spawned an apt definition of sin that I believe succinctly sums up our harmitialogical mess in a nutshell. Sproul said, 'Sin is not simply making bad choices or mistakes. Sin is having the desire in our hearts to do the will of the enemy of God'.

To 'save' people from their sins (by the way, it says 'from' their sins and not 'while they continue to impenitently wallow in their sins') entailed a multi-pronged attack, for The Son of Man.

First off, for anyone who dares to give Matthew, Mark, Luke, and John a legit and yet, mere cursory glance, you'll notice that Jesus had no *problemo* whatsoever calling out people on their evil junk.

He would rebuke priests and politicians to their face and oftentimes in public.

With His disciples, His 'chosen ones', He also had no problem at all letting them have it when they were acting the fool by following their foul flesh, their self-righteous spirit or the dictates of *el Diablo* himself, as in Peter's case (Matthew 16).

With the woman at the well He exposed her wanton life before He liberated her with His promise of 'living water'. And for the woman caught in adultery, we see Jesus not condemn her while at the same time tell her to 'go and sin no more'.

Ergo, to make Jesus out to be a soft peddler of non-offensive positive religious sentiments is to bastardize the biblical record that ubiquitously spotlights him doing anything but that.

For Jesus to 'save' the sinner he had to confront their sin.

For those who already knew they were wretched He offered them mercy, grace and forgiveness. For those who thought, 'eh, I'm not that bad' He took it upon Himself to show them that He thought otherwise. And for those that thought their poop didn't stink, He reserved His most scathing denunciations.

So, why did The Son of Man wield His incisive divine wit against the blissfully and sinfully ignorant of their true and dire condition? Well, he wanted to save them, truly, from their sins and sometimes, oftentimes, heaven's bad news precedes heaven's Good News.

This confrontational, politically-incorrect, course that Christ took is masculine to the core. Confronting sin in sinners is definitely not the *soup de jour* of the 'seeker-friendly' assemblies that populate our American evangelical horizon.

Why is the masculine task of rebuke and reproof avoided by pulpits today? Well, it's because most male Christian ministers would rather be liked than to actually save people from their sins. Jesus, on the other hand, couldn't care less if you liked Him or not and thus, He didn't mind causing people intense and internal short-term pain for His and their temporal and eternal gains.

Secondly, not only did he confront sin in the sinner He also paid for their sin by taking their well deserved death penalty and suffer The Father's wrath against *their* sin on the cross. That's a task that's not for the faint of heart. That too, is masculine to the core.

> *6 For while we were still helpless, at the right time*
> *Christ died for the ungodly. 7 For one will hardly die*
> *for a righteous man; though perhaps for the good man*
> *someone would dare even to die. 8 But God demon-*
> *strates His own love toward us, in that while we were*
> *yet sinners, Christ died for us. 9 Much more then, hav-*
> *ing now been justified by His blood, we shall be saved*
> *from the wrath of God through Him. 10 For if while we*
> *were enemies we were reconciled to God through the*
> *death of His Son, much more, having been reconciled,*
> *we shall be saved by His life.*
>
> Romans 5:6-10 (NASB)

Chapter 4

A Terrifying Toddler: Matthew 2:1-6

Now after Jesus was born in Bethlehem of Judea in the days of Herod the king, magi from the east arrived in Jerusalem, saying, "Where is He who has been born King of the Jews? For we saw His star in the east and have come to worship Him." When Herod the king heard this, he was troubled, and all Jerusalem with him...

... Then Herod secretly called the magi and determined from them the exact time the star appeared. And he sent them to Bethlehem and said, "Go and search carefully for the Child; and when you have found Him, report to me, so that I too may come and worship Him."

... *Now when they had gone, behold, an angel of the Lord appeared to Joseph in a dream and said, "Get up! Take the Child and His mother and flee to Egypt, and remain there until I tell you; for Herod is going to search for the Child to destroy Him."*

... when Herod saw that he had been tricked by the

> *magi, he became very enraged, and sent and slew all the male children who were in Bethlehem and all its vicinity, from two years old and under...*
>
> Matthew 2:1-6 (NASB)

Before Jesus formally stepped into his earthly ministry, when He was a wee little baby, merely cooing and pooping in his swaddling clothes and breastfeeding off the Virgin Mary's mammaries, He had King Herod try to kill Him.

Herod was an insecure, toady little leader, who was extremely paranoid that someone was going to take his authority from him.

Herod killed anyone, including friends, family, and foes, who he deemed a threat to his control. Google it if you don't believe me. His paranoia was the stuff of movies. He makes Jim Carrey, Charlie Manson, Zelda Fitzgerald, Syd Barrett, Vincent Van Gogh, Jussie Smollett, and Brian Wilson look centered, gracious, and easy-going compared to him. *Ergo*, when Herod found out that there was a male baby who was born King of The Jews, well ... he was having none of that.

Jesus' masculinity was a direct threat to the beta-male Herod's rank insecurities.

At first, Herod feigned respectful interest in Jesus but that was a hot steaming pile of *stercore tauri*.

Herod wanted to kill that baby because he thought He was going to eventually take his political position which he had connived so long and hard for.

Herod's supremacy was on thin ice with this male Christ-kid around, and he'd kissed too much Roman butt to let some Galilean grab his gavel.

Yep, this power hungry dude was threatened by a male baby born into the prophetic purposes of God, and the rest is bloody history, how he had slaughtered all the male children in the greater Bethlehem area just to get at Jesus.

Herod was the consummate, jealous/power hungry politician, who'd stop at *nada* to preserve his power. Kind of like the envious, soulless and specious political swamp critters on The Left and The Right who've made a very comfortable living off average American taxpayers during their near eternal feckless stints inside the Beltway. They too, don't want to lose their power, their control, their luxury condo, their mistresses, their lifestyle, their special interest mega-money, their CNN gigs or anything else they are clinging to and they'll come after anyone who threatens their dream, starring them as the center of the universe, with razor blades and lemon juice. Indeed, they too are driven by the same pathetic envious fear that saddled satanic Herod.

This war on boys, birthed to and bridled by, the eternal purpose of God has been seen before. In Exodus 1:16 Pharaoh ordered the death of all Hebrew male babies.

It appears as if wicked oppressors are always interested in undermining the masculinity of the oppressed.

Nothing suits a pathetic culture and political tyrants more

than their subjects' losing access to masculine role models filled with the warrior spirit. That's why they came after Moses and Jesus and why, The Left, in particular, are trying to eradicate masculinity from our culture and your son and grandson. And here's why: genuine masculinity is a threat to oppressive governments and policies that enslave people.

And as stated, evil leaders start when the boys are young.

Our current bevvy of misandrists might not be advocating for the death of boys but they sure as heck think that their masculinity is toxic and thus they're attempting to drug, shame and cajole them away from the God-given testosterone fog that The Trinity naturally hardwired boys to dwell in.

Pharaoh, Herod and today's man-haters know that the masculine 'seed of the woman,' in its infantile state, will eventually grow up to crush serpents and these *el Diablo* inspired control freaks can't have that now, can they?

Chapter 5.

Baptized Dragonslayer
Matthew 3:13-16

---

*13 Then Jesus *arrived from Galilee at the Jordan coming to John, to be baptized by him. 14 But John tried to prevent Him, saying, "I have need to be baptized by You, and do You come to me?" 15 But Jesus answering said to him, "Permit it at this time; for in this way it is fitting for us to fulfill all righteousness." Then he *permitted Him. 16 After being baptized, Jesus came up immediately from the water; and behold, the heavens were opened, and he saw the Spirit of God descending as a dove and lighting on Him, 17 and behold, a voice out of the heavens said, "This is My beloved Son, in whom I am well-pleased."*

Matthew 3:13-17 (NASB)

When folks get baptized nowadays, in your typical church, it usually entails the following:

1. The presence of friends and family looking on.

2. A livestream video feed via Facebook of the baptism.

3. A ton of Instagram pics of the event.

4. A post-baptism dysfunctional family luncheon at Golden Corral celebrating the baptizee's cessation from being a drunken, tenth-degree horndog, who used to take notes during Keeping Up With Kardashians.

5. Which is then followed by fifteen-years of the 'new believer' backsliding through lackluster discipleship that ends with them dying later on in life and finally getting into heaven by the skin of their teeth.

Jesus' baptism was a wee bit different.

When Jesus, at the ripe young age of thirty, was baptized he assumed the masculine role/responsibility of Dragonslayer and Temple Builder.

Oh, yes, ladies and gents, this was an official declaration that Satan's doomed and the Church Jesus is going to build and leave behind is going to ransack the Gates of Hell.

His baptism was a formal announcement of War.

Here's what commenced after Jesus' epic initiation into the Jordan's baptismal waters.

Number One. Jesus formally left being mommy and daddy's boy. I'm sure they were proud of their special son, but the relationship of Him being beholden to their familial hopes and dreams and his job as a carpenter was officially *over*.

Yep, from here on out it wasn't what mommy wanted that flicked His switch, it was what His heavenly Father desired that carved out His fresh, going forward, glidepath.

Can that be said about your life since your baptism? That you, too, have ceased to follow others, even well meaning family and friends, and are now hot on the trail of the will of The Father?

Number Two. Jesus ceased to be just a 'good guy.' Prior to Jesus's baptism He was a sinless nice young man. No one hated him. No one wanted to throw him off a cliff. No one wanted to beat his flesh off his body and crucify him but that all was about to change.

In addition, I bet no one really saw 'His potential' to be The Answer to humanity's sin-cursed condition. No one saw him being The Chief Exorcist of Devils. No one knew he was The Foundation Stone of the global Church destined to raze hell. Sure His family heard via Zacharias, at Jesus birth, that He was born to rock Satan's strongholds (Luke 1) but they had obviously forgotten about it because when he launched out, after His baptism, into His earthly ministry, his family thought he'd lost his ever-lovin' mind. Checkout Mark 3:20,21 if you don't believe me.

Indeed, the formally nice Jewish boy was now a rebellious

young man on a mission from God to destroy all things odious to His Father and that which enslaved His elect.

Number Three. The baptism formally moved him into the masculine role of Apocalyptic Warrior. His baptism was a cutting off of his old life as a sweet teenager and twentysomething, who probably won all kinds of awards in High School, to His new role as exorcist, miracle worker, truth teller, Pharisee rebuker, dragonslayer, temple-builder, and sacrificial offering for mankind's sins. And folks, all the aforementioned, which officially commenced when He rose out of the muddy Jordan River, is masculine to the core. That's a tough act to follow for dainty daisy 21st-century quasi-male Christians.

His baptism propelled into the masculine leadership role of provider, protector, hunter, and hero. He wasn't just going to tell nice stories. He was now going to kick major demonic backside and then crush the devil himself via his death, burial and resurrection.

And that all got rollin' right after his baptism.

Chapter 6.

Devil Defeater
Matthew 4:1-11

---

4 Then Jesus was led up by the Spirit into the wilder-
ness to be tempted by the devil. 2 And after He had
fasted forty days and forty nights, He then became hun-
gry. 3 And the tempter came and said to Him, "If You
are the Son of God, command that these stones become
bread." 4 But He answered and said, "It is written,
'Man shall not live on bread alone, but on every word
that proceeds out of the mouth of God.'"

*5 Then the devil *took Him into the holy city and had*
*Him stand on the pinnacle of the temple, 6 and *said to*
Him, "If You are the Son of God, throw Yourself down;
for it is written,

'He will command His angels concerning You';

and

'On their hands they will bear You up,

> *So that You will not strike Your foot against a stone.'"*
>
> *7 Jesus said to him, "On the other hand, it is written,*
> *'You shall not put the Lord your God to the test.'"*
>
> *8 Again, the devil *took Him to a very high mountain*
> *and *showed Him all the kingdoms of the world and*
> *their glory; 9 and he said to Him, "All these things*
> *I will give You, if You fall down and worship me." 10*
> *Then Jesus *said to him, "Go, Satan! For it is written,*
> *'You shall worship the Lord your God, and serve Him*
> *only.'" 11 Then the devil *left Him; and behold, angels*
> *came and began to minister to Him.*
>
> Matthew 4:1-11 (NASB)

Please note that right after Jesus's baptism He wastes no time, whatsoever, going toe-to-toe with *el Diablo*. Jesus didn't start a prophetic blog. He didn't ramp up His social media page with cool memes and glamour photos of Himself holding a cuddly lamb with a live link to the particular sandals he was wearing, or a sixty-second mashup video of Him turning clay pigeons into doves or changing Evian into merlot.

Nope, the Spirit of God took The Son of God to the woods in order to have Satan throw everything he had at Him and try to seduce Him away from the will of The Father.

That was a world class intellectual and spiritual jiu jitsu match, peeps.

Every punch Satan threw at Him landed in mid-air as Jesus adeptly bobbed and weaved His holy way through Satan's multifaceted wares.

Here's something that I wish ministers would tell their poor sheeple right after they get baptized: Dear So-and-So, now that you're a new creation in Christ Jesus you are now going to be attacked by the powers of darkness like cheap blouse marked down to $1.99 at Target's Black Friday Sale.

Yes, boys and girls, once you say, 'Yes!' to Jesus, Satan says, 'to hell with you' and the temptations and demonic attacks come in like a flood.

Indeed, you're going to get tossed into a satanic woodchipper that's been chewing up saints since Adam and Eve got tossed out of the sweet haven of Eden's crib.

Welcome to the Jungle.

It's time to nut up, shut up, and toughen up or you're not going to make it.

Look man, Jesus didn't have it easy. Why do you think you will?

Jesus waged war with the dragon and He did it with The Word of God.

Most typical Christians in today's easy-breezy, summer-squeezy, churches are biblically illiterate and are thus no match for the malevolent one. When the powers of darkness tempt most believers to eat their plate of lies, they not only eat it but they ask for seconds.

Serious Bible study is the stuff of men.

Tinkerpots don't read.

Tinkerpots don't think widely and deeply upon the Word of God.

Consequently, they're no match for the demonic hordes when it comes to the matching of wits and the ability to flee from Satan's multifaceted snares.

Jesus wasn't like that.

The word of God came thundering through His lips when Satan started yapping and therefore, He walked away The Victor instead of the victim of the devil's devices.

Oh, and I almost forgot, Jesus not only defeated Satan through the powerful wielding of God's holy word but he also did it on an empty-stomach. Can you say, 'masculine?'

Chapter 7

Repentance Preacher
Matthew 4:12-17

---

*12 Now when Jesus heard that John had been taken
into custody, He withdrew into Galilee; 13 and leaving
Nazareth, He came and settled in Capernaum, which
is by the sea, in the region of Zebulun and Naphtali. 14
This was to fulfill what was spoken through Isaiah the
prophet:*

15 "The land of Zebulun and the land of Naphtali,

By the way of the sea, beyond the Jordan, Galilee of the Gentiles—

16 "The people who were sitting in darkness saw a great Light,

And those who were sitting in the land and shadow of death,

Upon them a Light dawned."

17 From that time Jesus began to preach and say, "Repent, for the kingdom of heaven is at hand."

Matthew 4:12-17 (NASB)

I would be willing to give up my left testicle just to have had the opportunity to have heard Jesus preach while He was kickin' up dust on the mean streets of the Middle East two-thousand years ago.

Can you imagine actually beholding The Incarnate Word actually preaching the Word?

I don't know about you, but I hope they have videos of Him preaching that I can watch once I get to heaven because I guarantee that was some epic … holy ... stuff.

One thing is for certain: His sermons weren't muddy and murky, cheeky and cutesy, platitudes and maxims, built to make people feel good about being an impenitent sinner; deluding them into thinking that 'they're fine and heaven waits for them' all the while they're tooling down AC/DC's Highway to Hell at ninety-miles-per-hour.

The message that Jesus preached wasn't some lame, half-baked, seeker friendly, 'what does he mean', indefinable horse-scat that terrified pastors craft to keep in the good graces of the politically correct Thought Police who now threaten churches with lawsuits if they preach against their particular penchants.

Oh, heck no, Dinky.

Jesus' message was *repentance*.

It was, turn or burn.

It was, do a 180.

It was, leave everything and follow me.

It was, if you love anything more than me, then you're not worthy of me.

Jesus' message was, you're wrong … I'm right.

His message was, I am the way, the truth and the life and no one gets to The Father except through me.

It wasn't, 'there are many ways to God.'

Jesus' message wasn't the byproduct of a focus group of feckless friars trying to appeal to the carnal appetites of the damned.

Jesus knew hell awaited the unrepentant, therefore, His message was … *repent.*

Speaking of hell, as Dr. R.C. Sproul said,

> *'Its because Jesus spoke so frequently about hell that the Church should take the concept seriously.'*

But the Church doesn't.

Why?

Well, it's because the Church has become effeminized and has lost the holy and masculine fortitude to say the tough things that must be said in order to truly rescue dunderheads like me from their impending and eternal doom, if … they … don't … repent.

True men of God, like Jesus, will not dull their sword because their crowds can't handle the plain-dealing.

Effeminate, Nancy Boy pastors, however, will.

All the biblical greats, from the prophets, lawgivers, judges, psalmists, righteous kings, priests and The Chief Dragonslayer himself, Jesus, preached repent, hell-fire, ye must be born again, to whomever, whenever, they opened their righteous mouth on behalf of their Holy God.

And they didn't apologize for making people feel bad. As in, real bad.

The apostle Paul put it this way …

> *8 For though I caused you sorrow by my letter, I do*
> *not regret it; though I did regret it—for I see that that*
> *letter caused you sorrow, though only for a while— 9 I*
> *now rejoice, not that you were made sorrowful, but that*
> *you were made sorrowful to the point of repentance; for*
> *you were made sorrowful according to the will of God,*
> *so that you might not suffer loss in anything through*
> *us. 10 For the sorrow that is according to the will of*
> *God produces a repentance without regret, leading to*
> *salvation, but the sorrow of the world produces death.*
> *11 For behold what earnestness this very thing, this*
> *godly sorrow, has produced in you: what vindication of*
> *yourselves, what indignation, what fear, what longing,*
> *what zeal, what avenging of wrong! In everything you*
> *demonstrated yourselves to be innocent in the matter.*
>
> 2 Corinthians 7:8-11 (NASB)

True men of God, like Jesus, preach the hard truths of

the scripture that'll ruin your day but will, if believed and received, make your life an homage to your Creator, a true gospel benefit to mankind, while sparing you from an eternal deep-fry in outer darkness.

Chapter 8

Salty Dawgs
Matthew 5:13

13 "You are the salt of the earth; but if the salt has become tasteless, how can it be made salty again? It is no longer good for anything, except to be thrown out and trampled under foot by men."

Matthew 5:13 (NASB)

Matthew chapter five commences Jesus' longest message on record, the three-chapter, world-famous, Sermon on The Mount.

In this sermon, Jesus sets his sights high and wide in this demon rattling rant. Most people don't get how controversial this sermon was back in His day. But the religious hoity toities, that he aimed it at, did because they didn't like him too much after this speech.

Yep, the famous Sermon On the Mount purposely offended the self-righteous dorks of his day. It was bold, politically incorrect yumminess on steroids.

In The Sermon On The Mount, Christ defines what is "blessed" in God's eyes, how His disciples are to be in the world, Jesus' laws for relationships, what He says about anger, lust, cash, fasting, judging others, the proper way to pray, the stairway to heaven, and the highway to hell.

In Matthew 5:1-12, Jesus is talking generalities to the general populace. In verse thirteen of chapter five He turns His guns on His hand picked boys and declares them to be***... salty dawgs***. And he warns what happens if they, for whatever reason, lose their saltiness.

Please note, once again, that He called his disciples, *salt.* He didn't call them, 'My little sugar cubes.' He didn't say to His chosen ones, 'You're the pumpkin spice on the latte of life'. He didn't refer to them as, 'Jesus' jelly beans', but as salt.

Jesus chooses his words wisely. That's why He calls us sheep instead of porpoises. Why would He call us sheep? Well, we're stupid, we need a shepherd or we'll get eaten by wolves, that's why.

So, out of his vast vocabulary he calls the brothers, salt: biting, stinging, hot, dry, gritty, spicy, preserving, and healing ... salt.

Salt in Jesus' day, during Roman times, was worth its weight in gold.

If a quick history lesson regarding salt is on your Bucket List then I'm going to make your dreams come true right now. (* This is from Ian Harvey and Vintage News)

- What is SALT? It's an ionic compound made of sodium and chloride.

- Every person on the planet knows salt.

- Salt's profound impact on human civilization spans recorded history, and in fact, precedes it.

- It's been a part of human existence from our very beginning.

- Neolithic settlements, back when Pelosi and Biden were born, were formed around salt springs.

- Salt was essential when mastodons schlepped this 3rd rock from the sun and was in general use many, many moons ago.

- But this valuable item wasn't always easy to get.

During the early days of the Roman Empire, salt was used as a form of payment.

- Etymologists believe that the word salary came into use during the Roman Empire when soldiers were regularly paid with a handful of salt.

- In fact, this precious commodity was part of the reason the Romans built their roads: to move salt!

- In ancient Greece much of this trade involved an exchange of salt for slaves, and here we find the expression for a lazy individual as being someone "not worth his salt."

Back in the day, salt was *muy importante*. Some cities were formed and others destroyed in economic rivalries, sometimes even leading to wars over salt.

Speaking of War: The importance of salt in times of warfare can be seen throughout history.

- During times of war, national economies were strained to the limits and supplies of salt were often impacted negatively.

- This would lead to people suffering malnourishment from the lack of salt.

- When Napoleon's forces retreated from Moscow, many of the troops lost their lives as a result of salt deficiency and consequently, a low resistance to disease.

For those who believe in ghosts and zombies, there is the belief, shared across large parts of the world, that throwing salt on certain places or around the house can ward off evil spirits and even zombies.

Which brings me back to our text in Matthew 5:13, Jesus said, "You are the salt of the earth."

My paraphrase in the King Doug version of The Bible, 'Hey, dudes: you are crucial, you're valuable, you're gold, you're essential. However, if you lose your original purpose and power you're going to be an ineffective religious blob of nothingness and men will walk on you, ignore you, and you won't change diddly squat'.

Here's three distinctive traits of salt.

1. Salt frets, bites, stings, and yet … it heals.
2. Salt keeps food and animal hides from rot.
3. Salt's a spice.

Let's check out these three traits a little more fully, shall we?

Number One. Salt's a natural healer. It stings and yet, it heals.

God's given us a big job of healing the planet. Like salt, a true gospel delivery will sting before it heals. We want to 'heal' without stinging. That's not going to happen.

Like alcohol, another cleansing agent, salt will sting an open wound and cause initial pain before improvement follows.

> *17 "Blessed is the one whom God corrects; so do not despise the discipline of the Almighty.*
>
> *18 For he wounds, but he also binds up; he injures, but his hands also heal."*
>
> Job 5:17,18 (NIV)

Question? Why are there no messages about hell, sin, the judgment seat, our rebellious heart, or how we love to follow demons and darkness, how we hate God and the light and we are, by nature, children of wrath?

I tell you, 'why?' Saltless ministers have deemed them 'too negative' … 'too hurtful'... to the sinners' sensitive psyche.

The gospel and the cross is offensive to rebels who want zilch to do with a Holy God.

In order to truly heal them, the minister has to wound them first.

Never back down from saying non-PC, hard truths.

Without rebuke, reproof and conviction of sin, there is no true understanding of forgiveness, Jesus' sacrifice, grace, the wrath of God, and the penalty of an eternal hell.

Ergo, spiritual disease, infection, malicious bacteria continues in the church, culture, and politics.

All because we're afraid of being unpopular; stinging and being gritty when necessary.

Number Two. Salt kills rot in meats.

According to Howstuffworks.com …

> *"Salt inhibits bacteria in a variety of ways. It's a disrupter that wreaks havoc in microbes, interrupting their enzymes and chipping away at their DNA."*

It most often works through dehydration, removing many of the water molecules that bacteria need to live and grow.

Salting is used because most bacteria, fungi, and other potentially pathogenic organisms cannot survive in a highly salty environment, due to the hypertonic nature of salt.

In tanning animal skins, salting is what sets the hair and keeps the hide from decaying.

Our presence and our voice should kill cultural rot.

We should be a disrupter that wreaks havoc on satanic garbage.

Simply put, if rot's going on around us, we're not doing our job.

Number Three. Salt's a spice.

Food to me, that's not salted, tastes hideous. It's too bland. Matter of fact, wherever I eat, a salt shaker is nearby.

It's clear, from this analogy, that Christ calls His crew to be holy agents of change to this sin ravaged planet.

Also, we should do His good works with spice. No more bland Christianity. Be bold, life-giving, fun, faith-filled, hope-loaded, Don't be drab and dour.

Chapter 9

No Fear
Matthew 6:25-34

---

25 "For this reason I say to you, do not be worried about your life, as to what you will eat or what you will drink; nor for your body, as to what you will put on. Is not life more than food, and the body more than clothing? 26 Look at the birds of the air, that they do not sow, nor reap nor gather into barns, and yet your heavenly Father feeds them. Are you not worth much more than they? 27 And who of you by being worried can add a single hour to his life? 28 And why are you worried about clothing? Observe how the lilies of the field grow; they do not toil nor do they spin, 29 yet I say to you that not even Solomon in all his glory clothed himself like one of these. 30 But if God so clothes the grass of the field, which is alive today and tomorrow is thrown into the furnace, will He not much more clothe you? You of little faith! 31 Do not worry then, saying, 'What will we eat?' or 'What will we drink?' or 'What will we wear for clothing?' 32 For the Gentiles eagerly seek all these things; for your heavenly Father knows that you need all these things. 33 But seek first His

> *kingdom and His righteousness, and all these things will be added to you.*
>
> *34 "So do not worry about tomorrow; for tomorrow will care for itself. Each day has enough trouble of its own.*
>
> Matthew 6:25-34 (NASB)

I've spoken at, and have attended, many, many, 'Christian Men's Conferences'. Most, if not all of them, usually boil down to one message which is: 'quit masturbating.' Yep, that's what they all seem to deduce down to; namely, love God, love your family and stop whipping the bishop.

Seldom, if ever, have I heard the pastors, who chair these 'Men's Meetings', talk about the sin of worry which is a big sin in Jesus' eyes.

Matter of fact, in the aforementioned text, Jesus jackhammers those who wallow in worry because that vice eviscerates one's trust in the nature and character of God, The Father, and that ain't cool with Jesus, The Son.

When Jesus smelled worry, doubt, and fear in His boys he fish slapped that out of them, PDQ. To Jesus, worry was an egregious affront to the faithful love and care of The Father.

Jesus was not saddled with worry.

Why wasn't he?

Well, it was principally because he wasn't a tinkerpot and He knew and trusted His heavenly Father's rock solid dependability.

Worry is definitely not masculine.

Think of the pathetic and emasculated images that worry and anxiety spawn.

It's stuff like biting fingernails, chewing your lower lip, sweating like Adam Schiff at a Trump rally, fidgeting, tapping your feet and fingers nervously, jiggling your keys and change in your pocket while getting ready to bolt like quail on point by a bird dog.

Jesus didn't roll like that. He was bold in the face of Cat5 hurricanes, lack of food, no place to live, going toe-to-toe with *el Diablo*, hostile mobs, cruel beatings, and ultimately His brutal death on a cross.

Worry was not a part and parcel of His holy repertoire and He was not going to tolerate it in His disciples. It was a sin and when it manifested in His disciples he rebuked it out of them.

Instead of truly believing and trusting in the provision and protection of God, nowadays Christian men pursue what they believe will secure them, i.e., material things, 401k's, tribulation shelters, mommy and daddy, and of course Visa, MasterCard and American Express all the while numbing their anxieties with Xanax, Klonopin, Librium, Valium, and Ativan in order to offset their worries which the scripture calls the sin of unbelief.

Speaking of sin.

Much of the Church has a totemic view of vice.

The Catholics definitely do.

The evangelicals do as well but we haven't organized them officially under such monikers such as 'Mortal' and 'Venial' sins.

Within the Medieval Church's definition of 'The Seven Deadly Sins' worry and anxiety, which the scripture deems and damns as unbelief, isn't even mentioned. Hello!

So, why does worry get a pass from the Church and not from Christ?

I'll tell you why. It's because we all do it and worry doesn't have the scandalous 'buzz' sins like lust and wrath gin up.

Jesus rebuked His boys and exhorted them away from sweating the necessities of life like food, drink, and clothing, which were hard to come by back then as there were few grocery stores, zero shopping malls, no Papa Johns, or Starbucks, and Evian wasn't even invented until the 20th century.

For the uninitiated, food, drink and clothes were hard to come by for Christ's crowd. They were farmers and ranchers in an arid locale that could see brutal droughts and in the face of inclement conditions Jesus said, effectively, 'don't sweat it … God's got your back … He likes you better than birds and grass which are well taken care of and beautifully adorned by Him.'

Jesus said your focus should not be on fretting about such

things but on His kingdom concerns and He promised when your sights are locked-on to establish His will and way on the earth that God will float your boat.

Men, when they are worried, are refusing to trust God and thereby they let Him, their family, the church, and their nation down by curling up in the fetal position versus standing forthright, in faith, against everything Satan and life can toss at them.

Run from the sin of worry, my brothers.

Be bold.

Be strong and trust God in the face of adversity and watch your heavenly Father show Himself mighty on your behalf.

Chapter 10

Storms Promised
Matthew 7:24-28

---

24 "Therefore everyone who hears these words of Mine
and acts on them, may be compared to a wise man who
built his house on the rock. 25 And the rain fell, and the
floods came, and the winds blew and slammed against
that house; and yet it did not fall, for it had been found-
ed on the rock. 26 Everyone who hears these words of
Mine and does not act on them, will be like a foolish
man who built his house on the sand. 27 The rain fell,
and the floods came, and the winds blew and slammed
against that house; and it fell—and great was its fall."

28 When Jesus had finished these words, the crowds
were amazed at His teaching;

Matthew 7:24-28 (NASB)

'So what's masculine about the above?' I can hear the nasally critical tinkerpot carp. Well, Dinky, it's these three ditties:

1. Jesus promises pain.
2. Not everyone makes it.
3. His preaching had a punch.

Let's look behind Door Number One shall we? It's crystal clear, at least to me, that Jesus promises pain. He doesn't say *if* you get hit by a storm, but *when* you get hit by a storm.

In contrast to Christ's clear teaching regarding the promise of pain in this life, we have our current crop of ear-tickilin' … butt-kissin' effeminate ministers who lie to believers telling them once they say 'yes to Jesus', life will become an uninterrupted lite beer commercial of trouble free living, one of non-stop pixie dust and candy canes.

Jesus nuked that heretical notion in His first podcast.

Everyone gets a storm.

Everyone will have bad things happen to them.

What's masculine and refreshing about this promise of pain is:

1. It's nonsense free. Jesus forewarns folks of impending, could be calamitous, trials heading towards everyone who strolls this *terra firma* and they could be devastating if you've been playing games in a Christian Disneyland, not erecting your life on His

eternal principles. That's man stuff.

2. This shock-and-awe, reality based revelation, laid to the psyche of those who have ears to hear causes them to prepare accordingly and build their lives well. Forewarning equals forearming to the shrewd follower of the Galilean. Here Jesus is being a drill sergeant slapping His troops around and getting them ready to rumble in a spiritual war that's about to hit them in the kisser.

3. Effeminate pastors who love to be loved, don't brand their congregation with such an austere wakeup call because that type of intel thins their herd and they need that herd to buy their bunkum because BMWs can be oh, so expensive these days.

Another masculine aspect that Jesus leveled on the listener is something you don't hear too much of nowadays, namely: God is a tester and not everyone passes the test.

In our effete days of extreme wussification, we omit stringent testing of the kiddos in schools because they're deemed to be mean and could shame your stupid kid for being a moron who's been playing around instead of paying attention.

Indeed, in our times we give participation 'trophies' to clods who rocked up in 9th Place or ran the wrong way in a relay race.

Not so with Jesus.

He gives it to the crowd straight: The storms/test is coming and it will reveal whether or not we have built according to His word. If we have, then we'll be fine. If we haven't, well … don't blame God or your mommy … or anybody else. Blame yourself.

And lastly, Jesus wowed the crowd because He spoke with authority. His preaching had a punch and I pray to God that there's video in heaven of Him preaching back in the day because I would love to see how he preached compared to the sweeties today that fill pulpits around our nation.

I travel a bit, preaching around our country, and I'm disturbed by the lame, nicer-than-Christ, Sons of Charmin who're supposed to be Sons of Thunder.

There are too many that lack authority.

They lack gravitas.

They're like sappy Christian versions of Jimmy Fallon.

They don't scare people.

They don't convict the congregation.

They're puppets, not prophets.

They're echoes and not a voice.

They're not John The Baptist, they're Juan The Babetist and it is some sad and pathetic junk.

The prophets, apostles, and the Chief Dragonslayer Himself, Jesus spoke with authority. They branded the listener. They spoke on behalf of God, not a denomination and not from their fragile little ego that needs lukewarm sheeple to lavish mad praise on them because they live for the approval of men rather than the approval of God.

Chapter 11

The Untouchables
Matthew 8:1-4

---

*When Jesus came down from the mountain, large crowds followed Him. 2 And a leper came to Him and bowed down before Him, and said, "Lord, if You are willing, You can make me clean." 3 Jesus stretched out His hand and touched him, saying, "I am willing; be cleansed." And immediately his leprosy was cleansed. 4 And Jesus *said to him, "See that you tell no one; but go, show yourself to the priest and present the offering that Moses commanded, as a testimony to them."*

Matthew 8:1-4 (NASB)

These four verses from Matthew's quill spotlight three aspects of classic, biblical, masculinity that are evaporating, in many churches, like a pack of smokes at an AA meeting. .

What are they, you ask?

Well, I'm glad you inquired, you inquiring mind.

They are:

1. Jesus was a mountain man.
2. Jesus wasn't scared of lepers.
3. Jesus wasn't some little chick that bragged about what he did.

Let's chip away at *numero uno*, shall we?

Jesus was a mountain man.

I'll never forget attending a pastor's retreat in Texas many moons ago where I was publicly chastised during a dinner for ordering one Coors Lite.

That's one … Coors … Lite.

Not twenty.

Not seven.

Not two.

Just one.

I was told by this minister that I was being a 'bad witness' by drinking beer in public and that according to him, Jesus was angry with me.

What I found ironic was the fact that he was about two-hundred pounds overweight, had more chins than a Chinese phonebook and could barely walk across the restaurant parking lot because he was so out of shape.

Another thing I thought was a tad bit weird was him getting fussy about my one Silver Bullet when he had seventeen pieces of fried catfish and thirty-three hushpuppies. 'Physician, heal thyself' seems a befitting verse for Mr. Busybody.

If Jesus were alive today and hanging out on a mountain top old chunky butt would be left in the dust because of his self-imposed obesity and rank inactivity.

Men should be hardy and able bodied, like Jesus.

Jesus often hung out in the mountains.

Back then, there were no ski lifts or helicopters to transport one to a summit. Jesus had to be physically fit to get to these high places that he loved to frequent.

When most people think of Jesus nowadays they think of some pale-skinned indoor boy that hangs out with the Virgin Mary all the time talking about how mean the other boys are to him.

Most of the Christian art, which is total effeminate crap in my estimation, depicts Jesus as some squeamish, non-athletic, Boy George type dreamy savior who walks around in a taupe *peignoir* and sandals. In my mind's eye, I see the Son of Man more like a Bear Grylls, who has no *problemo* whatsoever traversing streams, bounding over boulders, scaling a rock face or piloting a gruff boat in rough seas.

Christian males, especially in big cities, wouldn't dare try to conquer a mountain because that would require sweat, getting dirty, possibly twisting an ankle or worse ... like wrecking their manicure they just got at Shambreeka's Nail Salon.

If you want your holy testosterone to kick in gents, get beyond the pavement, away from the lame and tame and interface with the wild just like Jesus did. It's magical. Be like Jesus and head often to the hills. Everytime he retreated to the woods He'd come back refreshed, filled with the Holy Ghost and ready to stomp more demonic skulls.

Another *muy* masculine quality in Matthew 8:1-4 was Jesus's willingness to interface with the forbidden lepers.

If you had leprosy back in JC's day, then guess what? Uber-religious people wouldn't go anywhere near you.

Not only did your ears, fingers, toes, nose, and penis fall off, you also didn't smell that hot and you had the added displeasure of lumps covering your noggin. In addition, to that humiliation you were banished to live in a Lepers Only subdivision that was about as appealing as watching Joe Biden and Nancy Pelosi dirty dance.

In other words, no one wanted their picture taken with you to share on their Instagram page if you were a leper.

Lepers were deemed 'unclean' by Moses in Numbers 5:1-4. Therefore, if you wanted to be considered Lysol disinfected by The Law of Moses and respected by the pretty people of the Old Order you kept the heck away from the lepers and the leper colony.

Jesus shattered that rule.

Following the New Covenant law of love, Jesus healed the audacious leper whose faith dared him to approach The Son of God.

Oh, and by the way, Jesus could have healed the dude with His word alone but He went a step further and touched him. That was completely unnecessary for Christ to render His supernatural power but He did it anyway.

In our current context the 'lepers' would be anyone who the legalistic evangelicals would deem 'unclean.'

Y'know … like peeps with COVID-19, HIV, meth heads, strippers, porn stars, the LGBTQ crowd, different races, political affiliations, and idolatrous cultures.

It takes a man to defy religious conventions, blow off what judgmental Christians will think about him, and reach out and touch folks myopic believers have deemed 'unclean.'

If you don't think that requires testicular fortitude then step out of your stained glass environment and try it. I guarantee it'll require *cojones* to ignore the naysayers and infiltrate unsafe spaces with the power and the love of God.

And lastly, Jesus told the former leper, *"See that you tell no one; but go, show yourself to the priest and present the offering that Moses commanded, as a testimony to them."*

There are two things I dig about verse four of Matthew chapter eight:

1. Jesus said to tell no one.
2. Jesus sent the 'unclean leper' to the priest for a little show-and-tell.

It takes a man not to brag about what they've done. Most pastors today would've drug that leper around the planet showing off how God has used them to heal this poor guy. They'd put it on Facebook, call up Oprah, and try to get Netflix to do a documentary about their mighty healing ministry.

Jesus, on the other hand, said tell no one. Jesus, you see, wasn't some little fame-seeking Christian tinkerpot. The only person JC wanted him to tell was the priest who deemed lepers as unsavory compost that shouldn't be touched but rather left to rot.

Chapter 12

Harvest Seer
Matthew 9:36-38

---

*36 Seeing the people, He felt compassion for them, because they were distressed and dispirited like sheep without a shepherd. 37 Then He *said to His disciples, "The harvest is plentiful, but the workers are few. 38 Therefore beseech the Lord of the harvest to send out workers into His harvest."*

Matthew 9:36-38 (NASB)

Jesus sees horrible conditions as a massive harvest and that's masculine to the core.

How's that masculine?

Well, instead of being a negative little Nancy, like many, Jesus understands the heart of The Father is to redeem this rabble and that where sin abounds, grace is there, in abundance, to crush it (Rom.5:20).

You see, when Jesus sees a tawdry mess, He doesn't curl up in the fetal position and wet His robe but rather boldly goes to the rescue of those ravaged by the powers of darkness.

A lot of chaos and pain means Mega-Millions in the soul saving department for The Son of Man.

Most of us, when we see a stack of people who're more confused than a termite in a yo-yo and are more befuddled than Britney Spears during a Dostoevsky read at Barnes and Noble think, 'well this is the end of the world.'

Jesus saw this depressed mob as prime Holy Ghost pickings for the Kingdom of God.

What made them look like low hanging spiritual fruit to Christ?

Well it was the following: They were distressed. Meaning, they were in great pain, anxiety, or sorrow. They were under acute physical or mental suffering, affliction and trouble, and they were dispirited. In other words, they were not feeling much hope for their lives.

When Jesus got an eye-full of this desperate throng He's like, 'Dudes … do you see this lost mob ? This is perfect! There's holy gold in them thar' hills'.

Here's what Matthew 9 screams to me: We don't need favorable conditions to do the work of God. Matter of fact, this pretty much says the more things stink the higher the chances of great success.

Look man, revival comes when things suck.

Miracles come when you need 'em.

Please note: Jesus said 'cruddy conditions' precede a great harvest.

When we look out at America, especially at our youth, most older Christians are like … 'I'm glad I'm gonna die soon so I don't have to watch Generation Snowflake elect Occasional-Cortex to be President of the United States.'

I believe if Jesus were tooling around this *terra firma* today He'd say the same thing He said two-thousand-years ago about our hopeless and hapless hordes, namely, the harvest is plentiful but the workers are few.

Here's five observations from Matthew 9:36-38.

Number One. Jesus sees differently than most Christians. Jesus sees a mega-harvest in hellacious mayhem.

My three-year-old grandson was over at our house the other day and we had a group of whitetail start pouring through the east end of our property. Within that group was a really nice free-range, low fence, Texas Hill Country, main-frame, eight point buck.

I could tell just with the naked eye that buck was a stud. I quickly grabbed my binoculars to get a better look at him and I was right. He was a beast.

With the buck still lingering under our massive oak trees, I gave the binocs to my grandson, Hamish, for him to have a look at the *muy grande* that had paid us a visit that fall afternoon.

After handing the binoculars off to Hamish I looked back up at the deer that were still milling around and eating acorns and I asked Hamish if he could see the buck. There was no reply. So I asked him again and nada. Then I looked down at Hamish and understood why he couldn't see that epic deer: he had the binocs backwards. I chuckled inside and then scooped him up in my arms and held the binoculars properly for him and he finally got a big eye-full of that trophy whitetail.

Most Christians look at cultural, political and familial problems with their biblical binocs backwards.

When they see 'bad signs' they think 'nothing can be done' and 'it's proof' God's about to run the credits on this failed earth flick. They believe in time, well … the devil wins and their only hope is to get raptured out of this mess.

Their Jesus is little.

Their faith is little.

Therefore, the zeal to work in inclement conditions is zilch because they see doom and gloom versus a Mighty God who is able to save in the roughest of waters.

Indeed, they see the devil and his anti-Christian minions as the winner on this planet, in time, and Jesus and His team only win in eternity.

Rarely will you hear a typical evangelical, when they are looking at crap cultural conditions, exclaim like Jesus did with a faith-filled affirmation that this 'hopeless situation' is actually awesome soul winning conditions!

Again, Jesus sees harvest in mayhem because He's not a defeated forlorn tinkerpot.

What do you see?

Number Two. Jesus feels differently about other people's pain than most Christians.

One way to know you're morphing into a self-righteous toad that Jesus loves to hate is when you can callously look out at people trapped in sin and are getting beat up in life and say, 'Well, that's what they get for not being a good Christian like me.'

I'll never forget sitting in one of my high school classes bragging about something stupid I had done that weekend and this carpy Christian chick said, without a scrap of love, 'you're lucky you're not dead and in hell'. What was the message I received from that denunciation? It was this: Jesus hates me.

Interestingly enough, there was another girl that too was very familiar with my evil path and she asked me if I knew that God loved me? I remember recoiling like Kramer would when he had his mind blown by something Seinfeld said.

What?

God loves me?

No He doesn't. At least not according to His people. 'God hates me and I owe Him money' was the message I received from 99.9% of the High School Christians I interfaced with.

The revelation of God's love for me, a notorious sinner, given with compassion by a lovely young lady was too much for me to handle. I didn't get converted then and there, being the idiot I was it took me another two years, but the message stuck. Jesus, who could righteously, justly, and without hesitation end my life and send me to eternally fry on Dante's hibachi instead extended love and compassion to me and I am forever grateful that He did.

The late Eugene Peterson, in The Message translation, morphs 'felt compassion' into 'his heart broke.'

> *"When he looked out over the crowds, his heart broke. So confused and aimless they were, like sheep with no shepherd. "What a huge harvest!" he said to his disciples. "How few workers! On your knees and pray for harvest hands!"*
>
> *Matthew 9:36-38 (The Message)*

You know it's easy to say, 'Awww. Those poor bastards' when you see someone flailing in life.

It's completely another thing for your heart to break over their plight. This is very convicting to me. My heart only breaks when things are not perfect for me and mine. Jesus' 'heart', on the other hand, broke over the distressed and dispirited masses.

This too is masculine to the core because it champions the

protective trait that's inherent in men who would be men.

God help us all feel compassion for others versus callous indifference to those who are 'dead in their trespasses and sins'. Because 'we too all formerly lived in the lusts of our flesh, indulging the desires of the flesh and of the mind, and were by nature children of wrath, even as the rest (Eph.2).'

Number Three. Jesus said this lost mob needs leaders/shepherds.

I love how easy Jesus made solving this big problem: His answer was two-fold:

1. They need leaders.
2. Pray that God would raise up leaders/workers to right this ship.

FYI, to all the indoor city boys: Sheep without shepherds are dead meat to predators.

The distressed and dispirited peeps need leaders … Shepherds to guide and protect them.

The problem is, effeminate, wussified, Christians don't want to do jack squat anymore but be coddled pastors.

Very few are looking to dive head first into the fray and lead people to Zion.

Nope, we want to be entertained and pampered, *ad nauseum, ad infinitum*. And then we have the gall to blather about how bad things are when Jesus said it could be remedied by folks who'll get off their butts and lead instead of complain.

Indeed, when it comes to leadership most Christians are like, 'It's not my job, man'. They don't feel 'led' to help, you see?

True leadership/shepherding is hard work. But it's what is needed in order to fix the stuff everyone moans about.

True men will heartily take on the leadership mantle.

Tinkerpots will flee from leadership. They don't want to labor for others' salvation because their 'Christianity' is all about them.

Number Four. in Matthew 9:35 (NASB) it says,

> *35 Jesus was going through all the cities and villages, teaching in their synagogues and proclaiming the gospel of the kingdom, and healing every kind of disease and every kind of sickness.*

He preached the 'Gospel of the Kingdom'. That's the message the workers/shepherds need to bring to the distressed and dispirited masses today. We need to preach and do the same thing Jesus did two millennia ago if we desire His kingdom results in our current conundrums.

Some of you are thinking, 'Yeah … and?'

Well, a lot of churches have deviated from the message and the acts of The Gospel of The Kingdom and have tossed that aside for therapeutic nonsense and politically correct psychobabble. Consequently, we ain't truly, eternally, helping anyone.

There are three things inherent in The Gospel of The Kingdom message: They are …

3. The message of repentance (Matthew 3:2; 4:17).
4. The healing of the sick.
5. The casting out of demons.

Question. When's the last time you heard a preacher, without apology, trumpet a thunder-clapping message of repentance from sin from the pulpit? Also, when's the last time, in love of course, you told a friend or family member they needed to repent/turn from their sin?

Here's another question. When's the last time during a Church service have you seen the minister lay hands on people who're sick and they get healed? Also, when someone's sick in proximity to your person, do you pray for their healing? That's what Jesus did.

Lastly, when is the last time you saw a demon cast out of someone? That long, eh? Is it because demons don't exist anymore? Or maybe they're not as active as they used to be? Or maybe we've strayed way off the essentials Christ preached and we're off doing our weird ineffective PC stuff that leaves people in their sins, with their maladies and demon possessed.

A true man of God preaches repentance, heals the sick and casts out devils. Effeminate snowflakes preach Oprah, sell the crowd supplements, and think ignoring, verses resisting, the devil will make demons flee.

Number Five. Jesus said to pray for *workers*, not the lost.

Here's another way Jesus differs from us: We pray for the lost and He prays for us to get off our butts and get busy.

To me, this is a hilarious contrast between what Christians pray for and how Jesus prayed for lost humanity.

Christians feel very positively pious when they pray from their Christian playpen for all the unwashed masses.

Jesus is like, 'they're ready to be harvested. Quit praying for them. They're good to go. What I would like you to pray for is for workers to bring them into my fold.'

Please note: Christ said, pray for workers. Real men of God work. They work hard and long. Effeminate dandies don't.

Chapter 13

Power Giver
Matthew 10:1

Jesus summoned His twelve disciples and gave them authority over unclean spirits, to cast them out, and to heal every kind of disease and every kind of sickness.

Matthew 10:1 (NASB)

Matthew chapter 10 is loaded with holy reality checks from The Son of Man.

It is rough.

It is unmistakable in its instructions.

It is clear regarding the tough path set before the true believer.

It is unmuddied on what it means to be His disciple and the

rewards of service.

It is filled with nut up, or shut up quips from the Lord Christ.

And, I guess, that's why I haven't heard it preached on for the last twenty-five years. It's simply too terse for the timid tit-mice that fill the pews in your typical sassy assembly.

This chapter is a veritable reality check on steroids.

If you were a tinkerpot hipster dandy who's into skinny jeans, big screens, smoke machines, Chai lattes, and being popular on IG this chapter will weed you out, PDQ baby.

What follows in the next four chapters are my brief notes on a big chunk of this epic chapter.

> *Jesus summoned His twelve disciples and gave them authority over unclean spirits, to cast them out, and to heal every kind of disease and every kind of sickness*
>
> Matthew 10:1 (NASB)

So, what's masculine about this?

Well, I'll tell you what is masculine about this passage.

Jesus shared His authority with His twelve *amigos*.

He wanted them to do the supernatural stuff just like He did.

Most insecure, effeminate Christian glory boys, if they have authority/power, don't want anyone else to have it because that might threaten their place in the spotlight and effete, solipsistic me-monkeys, cannot have that. Oh, heck no. It's all about them.

Jesus was a big boy, however. He knew He could get more kingdom accomplishments checked off if the twelve had His power versus Him just schlepping around and doing everything.

Like I said, most insecure males, who get a smidgen of power, want everyone looking at and praising them as long as possible.

Jesus, on the other hand, didn't sport a fragile ego. He wasn't threatened that someone might take His honor and therefore, He supernaturally equipped these rough and gruff first century fishermen with power over devils and disease.

You gotta be a secure man to give away something that makes you something.

Chapter 14

The Troublemakers Matthew 10:2-4

---

2 Now the names of the twelve apostles are these: The first, Simon, who is called Peter, and Andrew his brother; and James the son of Zebedee, and John his brother; 3 Philip and Bartholomew; Thomas and Matthew the tax collector; James the son of Alphaeus, and Thaddaeus; 4 Simon the Zealot, and Judas Iscariot, the one who betrayed Him.

Matthew 10:2-4 (NASB)

Y'know it's all too easy for the dialtone step-n-fetch American Christian to blow through that list of names and not realize, or rather, care that there were actual people attached to that august line-up.

One of the things I dig about Jesus' original crew is none of them were squeaky clean religious fundamentalists. Not only that, I bet most, if not all, of the pastoral search committees who take their cue from culture in selecting 'pastors' and not the Holy Ghost wouldn't have given these sunbaked sinners the time of day.

Oh, by the way, do you know what fundamentalist stands for?

You don't?

Well, I'll help you here.

It stands for 'no fun', 'mostly dumb' and 'quite mental'.

You're welcome.

Anyway …

Jesus chose rough cussing fishermen.

Imagine, if you will, the cast on the Deadliest Catch getting converted. Yep, these weren't dainty choirboys. They didn't wear cardigans. They weren't Mr. Rogers. These dudes were rougher than Grandma's breath.

These men didn't have the degrees you'd think they'd need to change the planet. God always chooses the base things to shame the wise (1Corinthians 1:26). God always chooses from the back of the line.

Look man, God can anoint a donkey, a hooker, a teenager, a whoremonger, an old geezer, an adulterer, a drunk, and a whomever to do His bidding. It's never about who we are, it is all about what God makes us to be. After these chap-lipped anglers went through The School of Christ for three years they were prime pickings to change the planet.

Oh, by the way, they were not the porcelain-skinned bearded women goofy artists have depicted them to be. They were holy troublemakers … world upsetters who suffered cruel deaths, beatings and imprisonment for the same Gospel that most lukewarm Christians living today take for granted.

What follows are the accounts of each of the original disciples' deaths. These accounts were taken from *Foxe's Book of Martyrs*, first published in 1563.

May God grant us a scintilla of their love for Jesus and His word.

> **Peter**. *Peter was condemned to death, and crucified, as some do write, at Rome; albeit some others, and not without cause, do doubt thereof. Hegesippus saith that Nero sought matter against Peter to put him to death; which, when the people perceived, they entreated Peter with much ado that he would fly the city. Peter, through their importunity at length persuaded, prepared himself to avoid. But, coming to the gate, he saw the Lord Christ come to meet him, to whom he, worshiping, said, "Lord, whither dost Thou go?" To whom He answered and said, "I am come again to be crucified." By this, Peter, perceiving his suffering to be understood, returned into the city. Jerome saith that he was crucified, his head being down and his feet upward, himself so requiring, because he was (he said) unworthy to be crucified after the same form and manner as the Lord was.*

> **Andrew**. *Andrew was the brother of Peter. He preached the gospel to many Asiatic nations; but on his arrival at Edessa he was taken and crucified on a cross, the two*

ends of which were fixed transversely in the ground. Hence the derivation of the term, St. Andrew's Cross.

James the son of Zebedee. *The next martyr we meet with, according to St. Luke, in the History of the Apostles' Acts, was James the son of Zebedee, the elder brother of John, and a relative of our Lord; for his mother Salome was cousin-german to the Virgin Mary. It was not until ten years after the death of Stephen that the second martyrdom took place; for no sooner had Herod Agrippa been appointed governor of Judea, than, with a view to ingratiate himself with them, he raised a sharp persecution against the Christians, and determined to make an effectual blow, by striking at their leaders. The account given us by an eminent primitive writer, Clemens Alexandrinus, ought not to be overlooked; that, as James was led to the place of martyrdom, his accuser was brought to repent of his conduct by the apostle's extraordinary courage and undauntedness, and fell down at his feet to request his pardon, professing himself a Christian, and resolving that James should not receive the crown of martyrdom alone. Hence they were both beheaded at the same time. Thus did the first apostolic martyr cheerfully and resolutely receive that cup, which he had told our Savior he was ready to drink. Timon and Parmenas suffered martyrdom about the same time; the one at Philippi, and the other in Macedonia. These events took place A.D. 44.*

John the son of Zebedee. *The "beloved disciple," was brother to James the Great. The churches of Smyrna, Pergamos, Sardis, Philadelphia, Laodicea, and Thyatira, were founded by him. From Ephesus he was ordered to be sent to Rome, where it is affirmed he was cast into a cauldron of boiling oil. He escaped by miracle, without injury. Domitian afterwards banished him to the Isle of Patmos, where he wrote the Book of Revelation. Nerva, the successor of Domitian, recalled him.*

He was the only apostle who escaped a violent death.

Philip *was born at Bethsaida, in Galilee and was first called by the name of "disciple." He labored diligently in Upper Asia, and suffered martyrdom at Heliopolis, in Phrygia. He was scourged, thrown into prison, and afterwards crucified, A.D. 54.*

Bartholomew *preached in several countries, and having translated the Gospel of Matthew into the language of India, he propagated it in that country. He was at length cruelly beaten and then crucified by the impatient idolaters.*

Thomas, *called Didymus, preached the Gospel in Parthia and India, where exciting the rage of the pagan priests, he was martyred by being thrust through with a spear.*

Matthew, *whose occupation was that of a toll-gatherer, was born at Nazareth. He wrote his gospel in Hebrew, which was afterwards translated into Greek by James the Less. The scene of his labors was Parthia, and Ethiopia, in which latter country he suffered martyrdom, being slain with a halberd in the city of Nadabah, A.D. 60.*

James the son of Alphaeus *is supposed by some to have been the brother of our Lord, by a former wife of Joseph. This is very doubtful, and accords too much with the Catholic superstition, that Mary never had any other children except our Savior. He was elected to the oversight of the churches of Jerusalem; and was the author of the Epistle ascribed to James in the sacred canon. At the age of ninety-four he was beaten and stoned by the Jews; and finally had his brains dashed out with a fuller's club.*

Thaddaesus, the brother of James, *was commonly called Thaddeus. He was crucified at Edessa, A.D. 72.*

Simon the Zealot, *surnamed Zelotes, preached the Gospel in Mauritania, Africa, and even in Britain, in which latter country he was crucified, A.D. 74.*

Judas Iscariot hung himself after betraying Jesus.

Chapter 15

Worse Than Sodom
Matthew 10:11-15

11 And whatever city or village you enter, inquire who is worthy in it, and stay at his house until you leave that city. 12 As you enter the house, give it your greeting. 13 If the house is worthy, give it your blessing of peace. But if it is not worthy, take back your blessing of peace. 14 Whoever does not receive you, nor heed your words, as you go out of that house or that city, shake the dust off your feet. 15 Truly I say to you, it will be more tolerable for the land of Sodom and Gomorrah in the day of judgment than for that city.

Matthew 10:11-15 (NASB)

If you've spent any time in an evangelical church that's worth its salt and you actually care about reaching the lost, I'm a guessin' you've probably attended evangelism courses about 'How to reach wayward souls'.

Some of these classes are good.

Some of them are bad.

And some are downright ugly.

In Matthew 10 we get a sneak peek into how the Master deployed his disciples in a daring soul-saving adventure.

I must admit what He charged His boys with is not what I've heard modern ministers give to their followers on how to reach the unwashed masses.

For instance: Jesus said …

1. For this outreach, it'll be Jews only (Matthew 10:5,6). How racist of Jesus, eh? If we were to target a specific group with our church's outreach, to the exclusion of others in today's coexist, kumbaya culture of political correctness, we'd get an ear full from Whoopi Goldberg and Pete Buttigieg about how un-Christlike we were. But here we have the Galilean himself saying, Jews only, for now at least.

2. The message Jesus' *hombres* were to preach was, 'The Kingdom of heaven is at hand' ie. God rules, Jack (Matthew 10:7). It wasn't, 'Please ask Jesus into your heart as your personal Savior because He has a wonderful plan for your life that'll unleash your full potential to be a better you.' Nope. It was God's rule has come and uh … yeah … you need to do this thing called 'repent and obey', por favor.

3. Please note, in Matthew 10:8 He also told his boys to 'heal the sick, raise the dead, cleanse the lepers, cast out demons'. His evangelism entailed supernat-

ural power encounters against demons and diseases. Does yours? No? If it doesn't then please explain, pray tell, why not?

4. In Matthew 10:9,10. He told his missionaries to not bank financial support before launching out to reach the lost. That's completely bass-ackwards to how our missionaries operate, generally speaking. Jesus, effectively, just tossed them out there without any cash. How rude, eh? How impractical of Him and yet, how effective that idea was because those twelve, or eleven actually, sans Judas, rocked the planet and they did it on a fraction of the cash the America church blows on it's outreaches. You see, what the early church lacked in funds they made up for in this thing called, 'The fire of the Holy Ghost'. Do you have that 'fire?'

Just those four ditties show how different Jesus was in His message and methods compared to our evangelistic efforts today.

The fifth element that is definitely not part and parcel of our evangelistic message is the epic chunk that lies in Matthew 10:11-15.

11 And whatever city or village you enter, inquire who is worthy in it, and stay at his house until you leave that city. 12 As you enter the house, give it your greeting. 13 If the house is worthy, give it your blessing of peace. But if it is not worthy, take back your blessing of peace. 14 Whoever does not receive you, nor heed your words, as you go out of that house or that city, shake the dust off your feet. 15 Truly I say to you, it will be more toler-

able for the land of Sodom and Gomorrah in the day of judgment than for that city.

Matthew 10:11-15 (NASB)

I think the last person I heard preach on these verses, especially verse fifteen, was Leonard Ravenhill and that was back in the late 1980's.

Very few 'evangelism teachers' tell the wannabe evangelists to include this jagged little pill in their soft and fuzzy 'community outreach'.

Let's break it down, shall we?

1. Jesus told his troops, only stay with 'worthy' people. 'What the heck is that about?' I can hear the PC-people screech. 'We're not to judge folks', saith the smarmy. Jesus shatters that myth by telling His boys to only stay with friendlies everywhere they go.

2. Give the house of worthy people your blessing of peace. Next on Jesus' to do list is once the *casa's* inhabitants have been deemed legit by God's standards, bless that abode with the positive sanction of 'peace'. This is very cool. Christ gives His ministers the power to positively impact a house, a whole family, with the peace of God. You should try that sometimes.

3. If it's not worthy, take your blessing of peace back. Whoa, Nelly! Jesus just threw us a curveball. If it turned out that the disciples discernment was a bubble off level and they got hornswoggle by the occupants of said domicile and they turned not 'worthy' but rather scurrilous, Sweet and cuddly baby Jesus

commanded the bros to snatch your blessing of peace back. Dang! That would not be 'very Christ-like' in today's evangelical world of wet goo now would it?

4. Whoever does not receive you, or heed your words, either the house and/or the city, shake the dust off your feet. Jesus doesn't stop there with just retrieving back the blessing of peace. Oh, heck no. He cranks it up to eleven and then breaks off the knob. Not only does He tell them to take back their blessing He then commands the brothers, in case the unworthy house is confused about what just happened, to shake the dust off their feet in protest of the unworthy peeps. In Italian mob parlance that act would be akin to giving the naysayers a big *fongool*. Some will. Some won't. So what. Move on.

5. Jesus damns the rebellious house, or city, to a fate worse than Sodom and Gomorrah on the Day of Judgment. In verse fifteen, the city/people who heard the Gospel and blew it and Jesus's messengers off are condemned, by The Son of God, to a fate worse than Sodom and Gomorrah. Please note: Jesus didn't give them a second chance. It was one and done. Pretty scary, eh? Also please note that those who hear the Good News and reject it will suffer more than Sodom and Gomorrah who never heard the Gospel. Yes, to hear the truth and reject it equates stiffer retribution, according to Christ.

And that message my friends, is masculine to the core. Most pusillanimous pastors will not touch that text with a ten-foot pew because they fear men more than they fear God.

It's too strong.

It's too repulsive to our cherished flesh.

And yet, it was Jesus' *modus operandi* for his boys going out on their first stab at reaching the lost.

Selah.

Chapter 16

Sheep & Wolves
Matthew 10: 16-23

---

16 "Behold, I send you out as sheep in the midst of
wolves; so be shrewd as serpents and innocent as doves.
17 But beware of men, for they will hand you over to the
courts and scourge you in their synagogues; 18 and you
will even be brought before governors and kings for My
sake, as a testimony to them and to the Gentiles. 19 But
when they hand you over, do not worry about how or
what you are to say; for it will be given you in that hour
what you are to say. 20 For it is not you who speak, but
it is the Spirit of your Father who speaks in you.

Matthew 10:16-20 (NASB)

Dear Christian: (Please write this down in your little teal-colored journal) If The Father ever calls you to truly do something for His glory and not yours, it's going to be fraught with serious danger and sick risk.

I beg your pardon.

Jesus never promised you a rose garden.

God never promised His people a cush ride.

Matter of fact, the Bible guarantees true followers just the opposite.

Indeed, as I already discussed in chapter fourteen, His initial itinerant ministers, save John and Judas, were all killed for The Message they preached and they didn't flinch in the face of death because they knew that was to be expected when one followed The Prince of Peace.

Jesus said, 'You will be hated by all because of my name' (Matthew 10:22a).

He said, '...whenever they persecute you' and not 'if they ever persecute you' (Matthew 10:23a).

Today's effeminate pastors omit all the aforementioned hooey because it is 'so negative.'

Instead, they put forth a faux Jesus who'll pay all your bills, get you a condo in Las Olas, a wife that looks like Blake Lively, a Lambo, millions of adoring fans and then upon vainglorious expiration, supposedly, your egotistical backside will be placed in heaven's chief seats next to Moses and Paul.

Yep, following Christ according to these heretical teachers, is quite akin to a lite beer commercial or hitting the Pick Six Lotto. Their message is just the opposite of Jesus' forecast of getting killed.

Jesus, on the other hand, told His men the brutal truth: I'm sending you out 'as sheep in the midst of wolves'.

The upshot of this 'negative news' is God'll be with you all the way and He ain't scared. God Almighty isn't rattled by any earthly threat from some punk human toad.

The same God who sent a nation of former slaves into the land of Canaan, a land filled with giant violent warriors, will send you, little Christian, into untoward environs where His enemies will come at you with razor blades and lemon juice. But we're to never fear because God is near.

Y'know, most people's 'Christianity' is way too safe.

Most Christians have never felt under any type of serious, viable, threat for righteous reasons.

A lot of Christians are loved by all instead of 'hated by all' (Matthew 10:22) like Jesus's true *amigos* were.

Now aside from the scary wolf promise that The Son of Man lacquered His men with, the reason He sent them into the woodchipper was to be a Gospel voice in the courts and synagogues; to preach to governors and kings for His name's sake.

In other words: what looks really horrible from an earthly perch is, in fact, an epic opportunity to declare the Gospel to this *terra firma's* gatekeepers.

Sure it's unsafe but, it isn't boring, eh?

Is your 'Christianity' boring? If it is you might want to check yourself before you eternally wreck yourself.

Here's how you can tell you're following the true Jesus: the enemies of The Gospel hate you.

Here's how you can tell you're following a faux Jesus: the enemies of The Gospel love you.

Following the real Son of God, according to The Son of God, is not for the squeamish.

Chapter 17

Disciples Defined Matthew 10: 24-39

---

24 "A disciple is not above his teacher, nor a slave above his master. 25 It is enough for the disciple that he become like his teacher, and the slave like his master. If they have called the head of the house Beelzebul, how much more will they malign the members of his household!

26 "Therefore do not fear them, for there is nothing concealed that will not be revealed, or hidden that will not be known. 27 What I tell you in the darkness, speak in the light; and what you hear whispered in your ear, proclaim upon the housetops. 28 Do not fear those who kill the body but are unable to kill the soul; but rather fear Him who is able to destroy both soul and body in hell. 29 Are not two sparrows sold for a cent? And yet not one of them will fall to the ground apart from your Father. 30 But the very hairs of your head are all numbered. 31 So do not fear; you are more valuable than many sparrows.

> *32 "Therefore everyone who confesses Me before men,*
> *I will also confess him before My Father who is in*
> *heaven. 33 But whoever denies Me before men, I will*
> *also deny him before My Father who is in heaven.*
>
> *34 "Do not think that I came to bring peace on the*
> *earth; I did not come to bring peace, but a sword. 35*
> *For I came to set a man against his father, and a daugh-*
> *ter against her mother, and a daughter-in-law against*
> *her mother-in-law; 36 and a man's enemies will be the*
> *members of his household.*
>
> *37 "He who loves father or mother more than Me is not*
> *worthy of Me; and he who loves son or daughter more*
> *than Me is not worthy of Me. 38 And he who does not*
> *take his cross and follow after Me is not worthy of Me.*
> *39 He who has found his life will lose it, and he who*
> *has lost his life for My sake will find it.*
>
> Matthew 10:24-39 (NASB)

You know what's weird?

All the bizarre hem-hawing one receives from friends, families, and pastors when they inquire about a church-going *amigo* whose life is a deep contradiction to the creed they crow.

Now, I'm not talking about a truly redeemed imperfect person who stumbles as they follow a perfect Savior but rather someone carnal to the core and they don't seem to care.

When one asks about the spiritual condition of said carnal Christian most mouths mutter something like, 'Well, he loves Jesus… he just hasn't made him Lord of his life yet.'

Well kiss my grits. I didn't know you could do that.

I'm afraid, especially in the American church, we've dumbed discipleship down quite a bit from the high bar Jesus set.

Aside from the egregious, aforementioned example, even compared with what Christ called a true disciple, I think we all pale in comparison to what Jesus deemed the fruit of the redeemed.

When Jesus defined disciple/discipleship it was pretty dang clear what the Son of Man meant.

Now, in our effeminate churches, being a good follower of Jesus simply entails wearing your church's T-shirt, sporting your church's bumper sticker, using your church's coffee mug and coming to your church's Sunday service that has effectively removed all offensive aspects of the Scripture while desperately trying to imitate Jimmy Fallon and The Tonight Show.

Yep, to most ministers, if a dude or a dudette does those four little ditties then they get called a 'good disciple of Jesus.'

I don't know about you, but I'm not looking to any man to tell me I'm a good Christian boy. You can get in a lot of spiritual trouble doing that stuff.

It's always the safest route to go to the word of God and have it judge you, define you, kick your backside and affirm you verses a human being because the scripture is an equal opportunity offender that only cares about the glory of God.

So, when it comes to what it means to be a true follower of

Jesus why not read what Jesus said himself?

In Matthew 10:24-39 Jesus doesn't stutter, mumble, bloviate or dampen down what it means to be His disciple.

Here's seven observations I gleaned in these sixteen verses.

Number One. Matthew 10:24-25 "A disciple is not above his teacher, nor a slave above his master. It is enough for the disciple that he become like his teacher, and the slave like his master. If they have called the head of the house Beelzebul, how much more will they malign the members of his household!"

True disciples shouldn't expect better treatment than what Jesus received and yet, most American Christians do expect better treatment than Christ because we've been sold a suffering-free Christianity by evangelical hucksters.

Yep, we've been sold a plate of rubbish that states if we're truly like The Son of God everyone will love us when the exact opposite is true.

The truth is, people called Jesus the devil and Jesus was crucified for a reason namely, He ticked all the right people off.

If … and that's a big IF … we follow the Spirit's lead then we, too, will attract the same animus of anti-Christian forces which thus, marks us a 'disciple.'

Number Two. Matthew 10:26-28. "Therefore do not fear them, for there is nothing concealed that will not be revealed, or hidden that will not be known. What I tell you in the darkness, speak in the light; and what you hear whispered in your ear, proclaim upon the housetops. Do not fear those who kill the body but are unable to kill the soul; but rather fear Him who is able to destroy both soul and body in hell."

Did you catch that? True disciples do not fear puny men who can kill their body but rather they fear a holy God who can destroy both soul and body, in hell.

One thing that characterizes huge swaths of evangelical pulpits and pews is … drum roll please … the fear of man.

Indeed, political correctness rules the roost in our, 'I wanna be loved by you' churches.

Pastors won't preach on certain topics lest they tick off testy entitlement droogies of the grievance industry who'll flame them on Facebook and Yelp.

Therefore, they're careful not to goad them versus being faithful stewards of the scripture.. A true disciple does not know such a fear.

Indeed, a true follower fears his final Judge more than they do the coven on The View and what they think about Romans chapter one.

Number Three. Matthew 10:29-30. "Are not two sparrows sold for a cent? And yet not one of them will fall to the ground apart from your Father. But the very hairs of your head are all numbered. So do not fear; you are more valuable than many sparrows."

True disciples understand that if God cares for a tiny sparrow, then He really cares for us and, therefore, we should be free from all fear and dread because an epic God goes before us and has our back.

Nevertheless, a lot of believers live in fear and buy a big chunk of the anxiety meds within the U.S.

We fear risk. We fear death. We fear losing a job. We fear asking a girl out on a date. We fear standing up for our faith in an anti-theistic environment.

We fear our wife's going to turn into Joyless Behar or our kids are going to morph into the next Miley Virus.

We fear Ocasio-Cortez will be President one day.

Okay … I've gotta admit. That is truly some scary crap.

AOC aside, just listen to most Christians … it's fear … it's caution … it's terror and it's dread 24/7/365 and yet we purport to be cared for by an Omniscient and Omnipotent God so … what's our problem?

Paul told Timothy in 2Timothy 1:7 that God hasn't given us a spirit of fear. Wherever we got it, it did not come from The Father.

We should take our cue from Christ and spit at fear.

True disciples' lives are characterized by boldness, not cowardice. At least according to Jesus they are. This should be the song we sing when we're beset with dread.

Why should I feel discouraged,
Why should the shadows come,
Why should my heart be lonely,
And long for heaven and home,
When Jesus is my portion,
My constant Friend is He;
Oh, his eye is on the sparrow,
And I know He watches, watches over me.
I sing because I'm happy
I sing because I'm free
For His eye is on the sparrow,
And I know He watches over me.

Number Five. "Therefore everyone who confesses Me before men, I will also confess him before My Father who is in heaven. But whoever denies Me before men, I will also deny him before My Father who is in heaven (Matthew 10:32,33)."

True disciples know that if we confess Him before little men, Jesus will stand by us before His father who is in heaven.

They also understand that if we chicken out and deny Him before men Jesus will deny us before His Father who is in heaven.

Which means, a lot of 'believers' are screwed when they take the big dirt nap and rock up to the Judgment Seat and go toe-to-toe with Jesus. And please note: the condemnation that Jesus will dole out to these dolts is not because they smoked, drank beer, went to Hooters' once, or gambled in Vegas, or thought that Hillary was an insufferable, narcissistic political hack, but it was because they went mute when they should've taken a stand for Christ and His word when it was unpopular. God help us all...

Six. "Do not think that I came to bring peace on the earth; I did not come to bring peace, but a sword. For I came to set a man against his father, and a daughter against her mother, and a daughter-in-law against her mother-in-law; and a man's enemies will be the members of his household." - Matthew 10:34-36

True disciples don't think Jesus was some kumbaya hippie peacenik. They know He came to bring a separating sword of Truth that'll sever family ties and make Thanksgiving dinners sometimes really tense.

Seven. "He who loves father or mother more than Me is not worthy of Me; and he who loves son or daughter more than Me is not worthy of Me." - Matthew 10:37

True disciples don't love mommy and daddy or their goofy kids more than they love Jesus. They focus on Him, not them. I'll comment more fully on this topic in my exposition of Matthew 12:46-50 in Chapter 19.

Eight. "And he who does not take his cross and follow after Me is not worthy of Me. He who has found his life will lose it, and he who has lost his life for My sake will find it". -

Matthew 10:38,39

True disciples die to themselves. They don't try to be a better me. They, spiritually, put themselves to death. They understand in losing their life for His sake, they find true life in Him.

Or as Eugene Peterson put it, "If you don't go all the way with me, through thick and thin, you don't deserve me. If your first concern is to look after yourself, you'll never find yourself. But if you forget about yourself and look to me, you'll find both yourself and me" (Matthew 10:38,39. The Message Translation)."

After plowing through Matthew 10, it is beyond me how anyone can deduce from this chapter that Jesus was some soft-spoken spiritual guru. This is masculine leadership and messaging, *par excellence*!

My next chapter, on Matthew 11, covers a verse that I can count on one hand how many times I've heard preachers preach on this text. Brace yourself.

Chapter 18

Kingdom Violence
Matthew 11:12

12 From the days of John the Baptist until now the kingdom of heaven suffers violence, and violent men take it by force.

Matthew 11:12 (NASB)

The aforementioned text is one you'll never hear preached on at your typical, Light-A-Fart Community Church's youth group.

In addition, you'll probably never hear a minister use that verse to set the mood for their Church's New Years' resolution.

Why do pastors avoid this epic text?

Well, it's too terse and too obtuse to the soft-focus, bearded lady, *faux* Jesus they've been foisting on their easily offended and indolent self-deceived crowd and if they run them off they won't be able to afford their mistress' Mercedes any longer.

So, *ipso facto*, this verse gets passed over like low-fat yogurt does at a Rebel Wilson plus-sized lingerie party.

If you think I'm exaggerating about the extreme neglect of this important admonition from The Son of Man by most ministers nowadays, then take this simple test: Go to your church's sermon archives and do a Matthew 11:12 word search and see if it pops up. Good luck.

So, let's dig into this little biblical nugget, shall we?

Jesus said, "From the days of John the Baptist until now the kingdom of heaven suffers violence, and violent men take it by force." - Matthew 11:12

When John The Baptist rocked up on the scene, as the emcee of history's main event, he was a holy wrecking crane to dead religion and evil politicians.

For four hundred years there was no prophetic word going forth.

God wasn't saying squat.

Until John.

And when John opened his mouth he shook all of hell.

John was a rowdy equal opportunity offender and boy howdy … was John good at his job.

You know what's disgusting?

Have you ever seen how the 'Church' has historically depicted John the Baptist in their paintings? Just like Jesus, they have made John look like a woman. Kind of like Mona Lisa's identical, very effeminate, twin brother. Google it. I dare you.

I countered their craven art with my own version of John in my oil painting series I've dubbed, The Biblical Badass Series. You can check it out via DougGiles.Art. I also did a short film around my findings that you can view on Amazon Prime Video. Just search Amazon Prime for 'Biblical Badasses: A Raw Look at Christianity And Art'.

John, like Jesus, was not some little twinkie.

When John preached you wouldn't go to sleep while he spoke.

When John preached you wouldn't wonder what he meant.

John left blisters on his listeners' souls.

John spawned conflict everywhere he went.

Where John trod he left a combination of riots and revival in his wake.

I bet today's pastoral search committees would 'pass' on asking John to pastor their Church because that brother generated nothing but solid angst wherever he went.

That first-century *amigo*, with his call to repentance, stirred up devils in every corridor of hell to such an extent that the only way to shut him down was to cut off his head.

And that's exactly what they did.

Jesus, in light of John's hell-razing ministry, said in effect, if you want to get in on what God's doing now you're going to have to get and stay, spiritually scrappy.

The Kingdom of God brings conflict and unless we're spiritually violent we're going to be roadkill under the wheels of satanic attacks.

John and Jesus were verbally attacked, physically assaulted, and both were ultimately murdered for The Message.

Half-hearted commitments to Christ won't suffice ever since John opened up his glorious mouth and let the devils have it.

The Amplified Bible puts it this way …

> *"And from the days of John the Baptist until the present time, the kingdom of heaven has endured violent assault, and violent men seize it by force (as a precious prize—a share in the heavenly kingdom is sought with most ardent zeal and intense exertion)."*
>
> Matthew 11:12 (AMP)

Did you catch what Jesus said was the violent attitude needed for one to 'share in the heavenly kingdom?' You have to see being on Jesus' team as a 'precious prize' that requires a 'most ardent zeal' and 'intense devotion'. And there went 90% of folks who claim Christ.

Question: How many Christians can you name who value Jesus and His kingdom as a 'precious prize?' Not precious in the, 'awe isn't that cute' sense of the word, but that which is highly valuable and is esteemed above every other person or thing or aspiration this planet has to offer?

Paul valued the person and work of Christ like that. Check it out in Philippians 3:7,8 "But whatever things were gain to me, those things I have counted as loss for the sake of Christ. More than that, I count all things to be loss in view of the surpassing value of knowing Christ Jesus my Lord, or whom I have suffered the loss of all things, and count them but rubbish so that I may gain Christ …"

Paul's affections ran hot for God. He did violence to everything that tried to seduce him away from the Father and His will. Yep, whether it was his lower cortex, me-monkey, carnal appetites or his self-righteous religious pedigree, anything that would tempt him away from Christ and Christ alone got the Pauline woodchipper.

Question number two: How many Christian folks do you know who sport a 'most ardent zeal' and 'intense devotion?' Who can be characterized as having an extreme, passionate, energetic pursuit of the things of God that is unrelenting in force, degree and strength in their love and loyalty to Jesus and The Gospel?

This is what Jesus calls, 'violence'. The person who has this is the one who gets 'a share in His heavenly kingdom.'

Make us 'violent', Lord.

Chapter 19

Who's Your Mama? Matthew 12:46-50

46 While He was still speaking to the crowds, behold, His mother and brothers were standing outside, seeking to speak to Him. 47 Someone said to Him, "Behold, Your mother and Your brothers are standing outside seeking to speak to You." 48 But Jesus answered the one who was telling Him and said, "Who is My mother and who are My brothers?" 49 And stretching out His hand toward His disciples, He said, "Behold My mother and My brothers! 50 For whoever does the will of My Father who is in heaven, he is My brother and sister and mother."

Matthew 12: 46-50 (NASB)

So, what's masculine about this chunk of scripture?

Well, it's simple: Jesus is not the mama's boy some

have purported Him to be.

In Matthew 12:1-45, Jesus is letting the self-righteous moralists, who think they're just peachy based on their religious performance, have it right between the eyes. He's thundering against their spiritual blindness and religious arrogance. It's truly an epic chapter of authoritative rebukes aimed at the religious ragweeds.

While Christ is in full stride, exposing the demonic hypocrisy of the uber-religious, speaking with Holy Ghost unction, there's a knock on the door and His mommy and His half-brothers want to … speak with Him?

Can you imagine?

'Hey, Jesus. Your mommy wants you.'

Can you imagine getting interrupted by your mom and your goofy brothers while you're delivering a divine, earth-rattling, speech?

Unreal.

How embarrassing, eh?

Here's a nifty little lesson: If Satan can't stop you by verbal threats from overt enemies he'll use a 'well-meaning' mother to try to derail your God-given mission.

Folks, Jesus was a grown man, on Mission from God, fish-slapping the Pharisees like no one else, blasting them with threats of impending and eternal doom and right in the middle of His scathing rebukes He gets a message stating, 'Mama wants to talk to you right now, young man?!?' You've got to be kidding me. What's Jesus supposed to say, 'Uh, hold on for a sec, my mommy wants me.' No way, Jose. That ain't gonna happen.

Oh, I'm sure they meant well. I'm sure they thought they were looking out for His best interests. Maybe they wanted to warn Him about the death threats He was under. Who knows? We do know His friends thought He was nuts (Mark 3:20,21) and tried to straight-jacket Him. His half-baked, half-brothers, did not believe He was The Messiah at that juncture (John 7:5). Yep, the folks who knew Him best thought He was cuck-oo and that He was taking Himself way too seriously.

So, I'm a guessin' Mary and the bros, out of legit, but mis-guided concern, were probably trying to get Him to chill out and dial down with ticking the whole planet off before He gets Himself off'ed.

Ergo, here they come, wanting an audience with Jesus, while He's kicking butt and taking names, trying to use their familial ties as leverage, but Jesus was having none of it.

Obviously, we know Jesus loved His mom (John 19:25-27) and His daft brothers, but He wasn't going to let them dominate His life like they might've done when He was a teenager. Oh, heck no.

Jesus used that well meaning, but rude interruption by His family to float a new Kingdom maxim namely, obedience is thicker than blood. He told everyone in earshot of Him, right in front of the Virgin Mary and His brothers, that the person who obeys God's will is who He considers family. Ouch, baby. Very ouch.

A true man, who follows a Holy God, isn't governed by what his mama wants but what his Father in heaven desires. It's that simple. As G. Campbell Morgan said, 'A boy will never become a man if he must always obey his parents.'

Chapter 20

Scary Stories
Matthew 13:10-17

---

10 And the disciples came and said to Him, "Why do You speak to them in parables?" 11 Jesus answered them, "To you it has been granted to know the mysteries of the kingdom of heaven, but to them it has not been granted. 12 For whoever has, to him more shall be given, and he will have an abundance; but whoever does not have, even what he has shall be taken away from him. 13 Therefore I speak to them in parables; because while seeing they do not see, and while hearing they do not hear, nor do they understand. 14 In their case the prophecy of Isaiah is being fulfilled, which says,

'You will keep on hearing, but will not understand;

You will keep on seeing, but will not perceive;

15 For the heart of this people has become dull,

With their ears they scarcely hear,

And they have closed their eyes,

Otherwise they would see with their eyes,

Hear with their ears,

And understand with their heart and return,

And I would heal them.'

16 But blessed are your eyes, because they see; and your ears, because they hear. 17 For truly I say to you that many prophets and righteous men desired to see what you see, and did not see it, and to hear what you hear, and did not hear it.

Matthew 13:10-17 (NASB)

Some people think that Jesus was nothing more than a well-meaning spiritual dude who told stories.

A veritable, moralistic, yarn spinner.

A righteous raconteur of some sort who wore a robe and Birkenstocks.

Y'know … a mystical version of Mark Twain, Will Rogers, or Norman Rockwell.

The fact of the matter is, He was/is The Son of God and not just some ancient cat who meant well.

Secondly, Jesus didn't just teach via storytelling. He also employed hyperbole, the Socratic method, humor, teachable moments and straightforward rebukes.

Here in Matthew 13:10-17 we have the first time, in the New Testament, that Jesus actually floated a parable.

Here's an FYI: When Jesus moved into an anecdotal, 'storytelling' mode, biblically known as teaching in parables, according to Him, it was to do one of two things: 1. reveal truth or 2. conceal truth. He was out to either greatly enlighten you or further your spiritual darkness. Aww, what's the matter? They didn't tell you that in the youth group?

Yep, when Jesus went parabolic on a crowd it was bad news for many there whose hearts were hard and had closed their eyes to the truth. Jesus said that some, because of their dull heart, would get increasingly worse under His teachings instead of better. And that my friends is some scary stuff.

Lastly, in case you missed, I'd like to point out that Jesus says God grants the seeing eye and the hearing ear.

You don't earn the seeing eye and hearing ear.

You don't choose the seeing eye and hearing ear.

You don't get the seeing eye and hearing ear because you don't smoke, or listen to Katy Perry, drink moonshine.

If you have the ability to 'see' and 'hear' … well, that came from the Godhead and it has jack squat to do with you, amigo. It's what the scripture calls, 'election.'

The elect, who do have their eyes and ears opened to the truth claims of The Gospel, according to Jesus, are blessed with abundant and ongoing revelation from Him. Those who're blinded and hardened in their stubborn heart just grow more and more ignorant and self-deceived.

To me, it is terrifying that Jesus would purposely employ a method of messaging that would actually allow for further darkness to overtake the hardened heart.

If you 'see' and 'hear' about Jesus' person and work, and if you trust Him and Him alone, for your salvation, you can thank God for that, because it wasn't about you choosing Him, but Him choosing you.

I'm gobsmacked by His grace on me.

Before He quickened me, I was dead in sin and I didn't give a rat's backside about knowing Him or serving Him. But the Holy Spirit karate chopped me, triumphed over my rebelliousness and changed my heart and enabled me to believe (see and hear) the Gospel.

And for that I'd like to say a couple of things …

1. Thank Father for your amazing grace and …

Again, I definitely contributed nothing for my salvation. As in, nada.

Chapter 21

The Miracle Killer
Matthew 13:53-58

---

53 When Jesus had finished these parables, He depart-
ed from there. 54 He came to His hometown and began
teaching them in their synagogue, so that they were as-
tonished, and said, "Where did this man get this wis-
dom and these miraculous powers? 55 Is not this the
carpenter's son? Is not His mother called Mary, and
His brothers, James and Joseph and Simon and Judas?
56 And His sisters, are they not all with us? Where then
did this man get all these things?" 57 And they took of-
fense at Him. But Jesus said to them, "A prophet is not
without honor except in his hometown and in his own
household." 58 And He did not do many miracles there
because of their unbelief.

Matthew 13:53-58 (NASB)

Familiarity breeds contempt.

That contempt can cost you your miracle.

And your soul.

The morons that grew up around Jesus in Nazareth, according the text above, lost out on a boatload of miracles just because they were familiar with Him and His family and couldn't square His current epic wisdom and miraculous power with His ordinary life from a sleepy little dipstick town out in the middle of nowhere.

In days of yore, Nazarene's were viewed as hillbilly rednecks. Mere country rubes and nobody expected anything good to come out of that one-camel town (John 1:46).

And that's a big reason why The Father chose a teenaged, unmarried, common girl like Mary from a one-stoplight town called Nazareth to birth His holy and only begotten Son, Jesus.

Nobody expected it.

No one saw it coming.

And that's just how God operates.

He uses foolish and common things and people to shame the goofy, religious, know-it-alls.

If you don't believe me Google, '1Corinthians 1:26-31'.

So what can we glean from this little Bible study, children?

Well, I've got three things from these six verses.

Number One. God uses that which is small and insignificant. He did with Mary. He did it with the town of Nazareth.

He did with Jesus and His humble upbringing.

Look, if you feel like a nobody from Nowhere going to no place, then guess what? It's highly likely that God's going to choose and use you greatly, my friend.

God loves using ordinary people in extraordinary ways.

If that's you, then cheer up dude.

The Holy Spirit's about to empower you to do mondo stuff for God and man. Believe it and receive it.

I'm blown away by how He has used me over the last thirty-six years. I was a pothead from West Texas who made Beavis and Butthead look like senior Mensa members. I was a veritable D- student, who was voted least likely to succeed. Indeed, I was a drug-addled goober who had to repeat my senior in High School and was kicked out of college and it was at that abysmal nadir that The Father scooped me up and brought me into His fold. When I was a base and corrupt no one, going nowhere, that's when He said, 'You'll do! Let's go jack with the devil, shall we?'

Number Two. When God starts to use you greatly, you need to brace yourself for the haters because they're going to come and try to neutralize you.

They did it to Jesus.

They're going to do it to you.

They're envious little toads that can't imagine God using you instead of them and they'll seek to level your influence and sully your reputation but you must pay them no nevermind.

Take a page out of Jesus' playbook and move on from those myopic trolls.

Also, please note, Jesus said your family and your hometown are probably not going to like God using you and will talk mad smack about you.

Number Three. Try not stun Jesus with your unbelief.

You can limit God, you know?

Jesus' homeslices did. They talked themselves out of being blessed by The Son of God because of their insecurities and unbelief that God would anoint with supernatural powers a young man that they all grew up with.

Wow.

Imagine that: God's not able to do many mighty works because, for whatever reason, someone chooses not to believe.

Question: When you're faced with a holy challenge, call, or difficulty, are you talking yourself into a miracle or out of a miracle like these first-century fools did?

Jesus said He did not do many miracles in Nazareth because of their unbelief. Put that on your refrigerator and memorize that verse.

Chapter 22

Water Walking
Matthew 14:22-33

---

*22 Immediately He made the disciples get into the boat
and go ahead of Him to the other side, while He sent the
crowds away. 23 After He had sent the crowds away, He
went up on the mountain by Himself to pray; and when
it was evening, He was there alone. 24 But the boat was
already a long distance from the land, battered by the
waves; for the wind was contrary. 25 And in the fourth
watch of the night He came to them, walking on the sea.
26 When the disciples saw Him walking on the sea, they
were terrified, and said, "It is a ghost!" And they cried
out in fear. 27 But immediately Jesus spoke to them,
saying, "Take courage, it is I; do not be afraid."*

*28 Peter said to Him, "Lord, if it is You, command me
to come to You on the water." 29 And He said, "Come!"
And Peter got out of the boat, and walked on the water and came toward Jesus. 30 But seeing the wind, he
became frightened, and beginning to sink, he cried out,
"Lord, save me!" 31 Immediately Jesus stretched out
His hand and took hold of him, and *said to him, "You*

of little faith, why did you doubt?" 32 When they got into the boat, the wind stopped. 33 And those who were in the boat worshiped Him, saying, "You are certainly God's Son!"

Matthew 14: 22-33 (NASB)

A lot of Christians nowadays believe that if Jesus calls them to do anything, it'll be safe, joyful, and feasible.

Indeed, following The Master, according to the mislead masses in our Gospel distorted American milieu, has morphed into a trouble free life of puppy dogs, candy-canes, a high paying job and toner abs.

It sure as shizzle does not … I said … does not … entail risk and possibly death, because our sweet and cuddly 'Personal Savior', would never, ever, place His people in harm's way.

Unfortunately, for the pusillanimous pastors who spew forth such sputum and the illiterate mooks who swallow that heresy and ask for seconds, the aforementioned verse blows that nonsense to smithereens.

Here we see Jesus, again, fulfilling the masculine role of provocateur, bidding old Pete to take a walk on the wild, wet side.

Effeminate and squishy tinkerpot pastors wouldn't encourage such behavior from their church members because, well, they could get sued for reckless endangerment which would lead to getting bad reviews on social media which in turn could cost them their $60,000 a month wardrobe budget and we can't have that now, can we?

Most ministers emphasize caution.

Most ministers emphasize comfort.

Most ministers emphasize political correctness.

Most ministers placate dull Christians inextricably stuck in their mind numbingly boring ruts.

Not, Jesus. Oh, H-to-the-No!

He will call us out into the Danger Zone.

Why will Christ call us to do the ridiculous? To attempt that which defies all good judgment? To walk on water?

Well, Dinky … He wants to grow our faith and it can't be done in the safe confines of the boat.

So ... Jesus calls Peter out of the boat.

Actually, Peter initiated the water walk. He probably got sick of sitting with the fear-laden screaming disciples who thought they'd just seen a ghost. So, Pete asks Jesus, 'If that is You, then command me to come to You on the water.'

And Jesus be like, 'Bring it!'

Please note: Jesus didn't say ...

1. No, it's too rough right now.
2. No, just row back to the beach.

3. Hang tight. I'll call *Baywatch*.
4. Let me rebuke the rough seas first.
5. Silly, Peter. You know that's physically impossible to walk on water molecules.

Jesus was like, 'let's roll Peter. If you've got the balls to do it, then by all means … do it.' And boom … off Peter went walking on water!

A Lot of folks bring up how Peter's 'little faith' caused him to sink. Which is easy for peeps who've never gotten out of their 'boat' and try to water walk.

At least Peter went for it.

At least he tried.

At least it is on his resume as having walked on water.

What the heck have most Christians tried lately that is risky?

Finally, Jesus, acting masculine again, not only bidded Peter to walk on water but He also busted his chops for having little faith and doubting.

You'd think Jesus would have high fived Peter, praised Peter, and/or bought Peter a beer when they got back in town but no … He rebukes him for letting fear and unbelief wreck his wild water walk.

And that my friends is what Jesus would do.

Chapter 23

Yo', Dawg
Matthew 15:21-28

21 Jesus went away from there, and withdrew into the district of Tyre and Sidon. 22 And a Canaanite woman from that region came out and began to cry out, saying, "Have mercy on me, Lord, Son of David; my daughter is cruelly demon-possessed." 23 But He did not answer her a word. And His disciples came and implored Him, saying, "Send her away, because she keeps shouting at us." 24 But He answered and said, "I was sent only to the lost sheep of the house of Israel." 25 But she came and began to bow down before Him, saying, "Lord, help me!" 26 And He answered and said, "It is not good to take the children's bread and throw it to the dogs." 27 But she said, "Yes, Lord; but even the dogs feed on the crumbs which fall from their masters' table." 28 Then Jesus said to her, "O woman, your faith is great; it shall be done for you as you wish." And her daughter was healed at once.

Matthew 15:21-28 (NASB)

Can you imagine if Jesus were here today, in bodily form, and He floated that 'dog' insult to a hurting female minority in our 'woke,' hashtag, immediately offended 21st-century social media scene?

Holy guacamole, Batman.

Today's online lynch mob would expedite His crucifixion, PDQ. There'd be no three-year earthly ministry after He played that derisive dig.

Maybe three months.

Tops.

For certain, the keyboard-ragers would demand that God, The Father, fire Him immediately from being Lord and Savior and require Jesus to spend at least a twelve-month stint being re-educated at The Syrophoenician School Of Sensitivity before He's ever allowed to show His face again, and that would be on Oprah where He'd trip over Himself apologizing to the planet with a sad, 'Michael Cohen before Congress,' look upon His face. Right after that, He would then have to forever prove that He's officially one of the woke by starting a 501(c)3 organization with Alyssa Milano that provides shelter, Sloppy Joe's, and free exorcisms for Syrophoenician women who have kids who're full of the devil.

Yep, I think today's Thought Police would swallow their whistle, hyperventilating, trying to blow 'foul, foul, foul' at The Nazarene if He were to launch that verbal missile at some needy female minority who's currently cruisin' this blue marble.

For giggles, let's breakdown Matthew's take on one of The Son of God's most 'shocking insults.'

Jesus, after rebuking the spiritually blind religious leaders and having to deal with His daft disciples (Matthew 15:1-20), looks for a place to chill and bumps into a non-Jewish lady screaming for Him to cast demons out of her daughter who's acting like Miley Cyrus.

The lady cries out for mercy and Jesus, seemingly, blows her off.

Jesus' boys tell Him to get rid of her because she's making too much noise.

Jesus then informs the lady that He's not dolling out favors for her kind but for Jews only.

The woman, undaunted at His rebuff, presses in for His help. At this juncture, Jesus jabs her with the dog jibe ... "It is not good to take the children's bread and throw it to the dogs."

Strangely, the lady didn't call TMZ or go on Twitter and Facebook and report a 'hate crime' and hashtag the MeToo movement for support. What she did do was extend His riddle by replying, "Yes, Lord; but even the dogs feed on the crumbs which fall from their masters' table" and walked off impressing Christ with her answer and in turn, He healed her kid.

No matter how theologians and pastors try to clean this text up, the fact remains that sweet and cuddly Jesus called this chick a dog. A vomit-eating, crotch-licking, butt-sniffing dog.

Dogs, back in Jesus' day, weren't these bedazzled, four-legged accoutrements the Real Housewives of Orange County carry to the bar nowadays when they go get wasted with their abhorrent buddies.

Nope, dogs weren't worshiped in ancient times. Nobody back then gave a crap about a one-eyed, lonely and hungry, cold dog that needed rescuing even if Sarah McLachlan tried to guilt trip them into adopting one by crooning, In the arms of the angel. Matter of fact, in the Old Testament ...

Smacking a dog was quasi-normative (1 Samuel 17:43; Proverbs 26:17).

Dogs in the OT were like turkey buzzards, in that they didn't mind at all scarfing down dead bodies (1 Kings 14:11; 16:4; 21:19, 23-24; 22:38; 2 Kings 9:10, 36).

Ergo, calling someone a dog was not flattering (Exodus 22:31; Deuteronomy 23:18; 1 Samuel 24:14; 2 Samuel 3:8; 9:8; 2 Kings 8:13; Proverbs 26:11; Ecclesiastes 9:4).

In addition, in the New Testament, calling one a dog equated to being considered one of *El Diablo*'s buddies (Philippians 3:2; Revelation 22:15).

So, why did I pick this text to display Christ's crassness? Well, it's principally because everyone gets Jesus laying into the Pharisees, crooked politicians or His disciples when they were acting the fool, but not Him busting the chops of a needy female foreigner. That's not very 'Christ-like' according to our politically correct culture that's been cowed by, and now beholden to, the grievance industry.

Chapter 24

One Of The Prophets
Matthew 16:13-17

---

13 Now when Jesus came into the district of Caesarea
Philippi, He was asking His disciples, "Who do people
say that the Son of Man is?" 14 And they said, "Some
say John the Baptist; and others, Elijah; but still oth-
*ers, Jeremiah, or one of the prophets." 15 He *said to*
them, "But who do you say that I am?" 16 Simon Peter
answered, "You are the Christ, the Son of the living
God." 17 And Jesus said to him, "Blessed are you, Si-
mon Barjona, because flesh and blood did not reveal
this to you, but My Father who is in heaven."

Matthew 16:13-17 (NASB)

What a great block of scripture, eh?

Thanks to Matthew, we get to eavesdrop on some backstage dialogue between Jesus and His chosen *amigos*.

At this juncture, Jesus is well into His wrecking crane ministry of rebuking foul and odious religion spawned by the scriptures ultimate bad guys, The Pharisees.

As you can imagine, the self righteous ain't digging Him at all, but the rubes and scalawags, spurned by holier-than-thous, are McLovin' what Jesus be doin' by exposing their glaring hypocrisy.

Jesus is creating an epic wake.

People are talking now.

He's getting a 'reputation'.

So, Jesus asks His disciples, 'What's the buzz on the street about me? Who are they comparing me to?' (Author's paraphrase)

The boys yield up three specific biblical characters and one particular ministerial function that first-century folks were comparing Christ with.

They were saying The Son of Man was either ...

1. John The Baptist.
2. Jeremiah.
3. Elijah.
4. One of the prophets.

What do all the aforementioned people have in common?

Well, my little children, they're all masculine biblical badasses, that's 'what' and that's exactly the vibe people were getting off Jesus' ministry.

Sure they missed that He is the Christ, the Son of the living God, but they didn't miss how He rolled namely, as a prophet.

For those dullards amongst us, who aren't familiar with the prophets because they're too lazy to read, allow me to school you regarding their powerful and poignant role in God's economy.

A proper, biblical prophet was unowned, unmanipulated, unbeholden, unbowed, undomesticated, unapologetic, and unashamed of God and God help you if you were on the wrong side of God's business, as God's people, if you ever ran into a prophet.

The prophet smashed religious idols.

The prophet challenged the spiritually smug.

The prophet blasted crooked politicians.

The prophet was politically incorrect.

The prophet mocked empty and stale state symbolism.

The prophet foretold pending doom and judgment.

The prophet's message was always, 'repent.'

The prophet could not be bought.

The prophet would wreck your world, to save your world.

The prophet was mocked by men and praised by God.

The prophet made no uncertain sound.

The prophet's words struck with the force of a sledge hammer.

The prophet's rebuke would haunt the hearer until they turned and followed God fully.

And that, my friends, is 'who' people were likening Jesus to.

A *muy* bold prophet.

Please note, how different the description of Jesus, by His contemporaries who actually saw Him minister, is to how He's being described today in our effete evangelical world.

Today our make believe Jesus would be likened to …

1. Oprah.
2. Mr. Rogers.
3. Brad Pitt
4. Paul McCartney

Y'know, politically correct, sweet and not offensive like a mangy, Old Testament prophet.

Obviously the focal point of Matthew 16 is the revelation the Father gave Simon Peter regarding Jesus being, 'the Christ, the Son of the Living God' and not just a powerful, yet fallible, prophetic human being.

But I, obviously, think it is interesting, especially in our evangelical milquetoast milieu where we've created a Christ that's actually nicer than the One in the scripture, that Jesus, during His earthly ministry, was likened to an Old Testament prophet instead of a pusillanimous, buttkissing, puppet.

Chapter 25

Faithless & Lousy
Matthew 17:14-21

14 When they came to the crowd, a man came up to
Jesus, falling on his knees before Him and saying, 15
"Lord, have mercy on my son, for he is a lunatic and
is very ill; for he often falls into the fire and often into
the water. 16 I brought him to Your disciples, and they
could not cure him." 17 And Jesus answered and said,
"You unbelieving and perverted generation, how long
shall I be with you? How long shall I put up with you?
Bring him here to Me." 18 And Jesus rebuked him, and
the demon came out of him, and the boy was cured at
once.

19 Then the disciples came to Jesus privately and said,
*"Why could we not drive it out?" 20 And He *said to*
them, "Because of the littleness of your faith; for tru-
ly I say to you, if you have faith the size of a mustard
seed, you will say to this mountain, 'Move from here to
there,' and it will move; and nothing will be impossi-
ble to you. 21 [But this kind does not go out except by
prayer and fasting."

Matthew 17:14-21 (NASB)

Can you imagine if Jesus were around today, in physical form, and He lambasted a stack of feckless pastors because they couldn't cast out a demon out of a naughty boy?

OMG, baby.

Jesus would be in trouble because nowadays our make believe squishy Jesus would never say anything embarrassing or untoward towards vapid, well meaning, ministers.

No doubt, if Christ were here and He let genteel Christian leaders verbally have it right between the eyes for being powerless wussies, He would be reprimanded, reeducated and/or swiftly fired from His role as Executive Pastor of, 'Aren't We All Just Precious Community Church'.

The real Jesus was rough on His boys.

No matter how you slice it.

He … was … rough … on … His … boys.

Again, in today's soft-focused, everyone gets a trophy Christendom, the Jesus who upbraided the disciples in Matthew 17:17-21 as unbelieving chuckleheads would come off as an 'irate meanie.'

So, why was the Son of Man more than miffed at His mealy-mouthed ministers?

Well, I think, and I could be wrong, that He had this thing called 'reasonable expectations' for His followers to actually move in the miraculous authority that they saw in Him and of which He had given to them (Matthew 10:1-8). Hello.

So, what, pray tell, did the disciples see and hear that old meanie Jesus was expecting them to emulate?

It was amazing stuff like …

- A leper got healed in Matthew 8:4

- A Centurion's servant got healed with just a word from The Master in Matthew 8:5-13.

- In Matthew 8:14-17 lots of people got healed and demons were flying out of folks like bats.

- They saw Jesus rebuke a thunderstorm in Matthew 8:23-27.

- In Matthew 8:28-34 they watched Jesus exorcise two more demons.

- In Matthew 9:1-8 Jesus heals a paralyzed dude.

- In Matthew 9:18-26 Jesus raises Jairus' daughter from the dead.

- In Matthew 9:27-34 Jesus heals a blind fellow.

- In Matthew 10:1-8 Jesus gave His disciples power to heal sick, cast out devils and even raise the dead and they went about doing it. Even Judas.

- In Matthew 12:1-14 the disciples watch Jesus heal a man with a shriveled hand.

- In Matthew 12:22-28 a blind and mute demoniac gets the devil cast out of him by Jesus.

- In Matthew 14:13-21 Jesus miraculously fed 5000+ people with five sardines and two biscuits.
- In Matthew 14:22-33 the disciples watched Jesus and Peter walk on water during a flippin' storm.
- In Matthew 14:34-36 Jesus performs even more healings.
- In Matthew 15:21-28 they watched Jesus cast the devil out of a Canaanite woman's daughter who was acting like Miley Virus.
- In Matthew 15:32-39 they watched Jesus, again, miraculously feed thousands of people.
- In Matthew 16:19 Jesus gave them power to bind devils and loose/release the power of God.
- In Matthew 17:1-8 Jesus is transfigured right in front of Peter, James and John and accompanying Christ in His transfiguration is Moses and Elijah!

The disciples witnessed and even personally partook (Matthew 10:1-8) in these spectacular power displays by Jesus over sickness, disease, demons and even death and yet, when they met a little boy with an out-of-control demon in him, they were unable to tell it to get lost.

Unreal and yet … too real.

And that, my friends, ticked Jesus off.

Oh, by the way, He did not mildly chastise His disciples.

He called them names.

Bad names.

He called them unbelieving (faithless) and perverted (twisted or lousy)

At thirty-three years of age, Jesus said He was fed up with the disciples and He'd only been with them for a little under three years. That's what sassy ministers would call, 'impatience'. It's what the Bible calls, 'righteous indignation.'

Not too many pastors preach about that side of Jesus. The 'I can't believe you still don't get it' side of Christ, and yet, we see it several times in the Gospels.

So, why the rage from the Prince of Peace at His chosen twelve *amigos*?

I think it was chiefly because Jesus had high hopes for His boys.

He was going to take these nobodies (his disciples) and shame the somebodies (the religious hoity-toities) and set the world on fire via these former rough cussing fishermen but currently … um … uh … yeah … they're not looking so hot.

Indeed, and in chapter seventeen of Matthew, Jesus is headed towards His crucifixion and He's attempting to bring them to speed prior to His departure and it's like they keep on flunking 3rd Grade and that's freaking Him out. And I dig this about the real Christ.

The Christ you hear preached/described today has no real worldchanging hopes in us.

He's just our Celestial bellhop to run our selfish errands and make all our dreams come true.

He is never disappointed in us.

He would never say nary a bad word about us.

Everything is just peachy and we're all fine and He's fine and yet, anyone with a lick of sense knows that twaddle doesn't square with this thing called, 'the scripture.'

It cannot be fine when demons drive big chunks of the church, culture, and politics.

It cannot be fine when 100,000 souls per day drop into hell and we stand powerless before such a flood, mouths agape, eating nachos, singing kumbaya, as we watch it go down.

I think Jesus would be ticked off at us as well because He, too, has given us the tools to tackle the powers of darkness and yet we stand powerless before an entire generation that is getting tossed around by demonic forces not just into 'fire and water' but into filth and wantonness.

I'm sure the disciples felt like crap after Jesus called them faithless and lousy and you what? That's okay. Sometimes we need that reality check.

Chapter 26

Handed Over To The Torturers. Matthew 18:21-35

---

*21 Then Peter came and said to Him, "Lord, how often shall my brother sin against me and I forgive him? Up to seven times?" 22 Jesus *said to him, "I do not say to you, up to seven times, but up to seventy times seven.*

23 "For this reason the kingdom of heaven may be compared to a king who wished to settle accounts with his slaves. 24 When he had begun to settle them, one who owed him ten thousand talents was brought to him. 25 But since he did not have the means to repay, his lord commanded him to be sold, along with his wife and children and all that he had, and repayment to be made. 26 So the slave fell to the ground and prostrated himself before him, saying, 'Have patience with me and I will repay you everything.' 27 And the lord of that slave felt compassion and released him and forgave him the debt. 28 But that slave went out and found one of his fellow slaves who owed him a hundred denarii; and he seized him and began to choke him, saying, 'Pay back what you owe.' 29 So his fellow slave fell to the ground and began to plead with him, saying, 'Have *patience with me and I will repay you.' 30 But he was unwilling and went and threw him in prison until he should pay back what was owed. 31 So when his fellow slaves saw what had happened, they were deeply grieved and came and reported to their lord all that had happened. 32 Then summoning him, his lord *said to him, 'You wicked slave, I forgave you all that debt because you pleaded with me. 33 Should you not also have had mercy on your fellow slave, in the same way that I had mercy on you?' 34 And his lord, moved with anger, handed him over to the torturers until he should repay all that was owed him. 35 My heavenly Father will also do the same to you, if each of you does not forgive his brother from your heart."*

Matthew 18:21-35 (NASB)

It's wild how unforgiving Christians can become.

I know some believers who'd never drink a beer, smoke a cigar, watch a Quentin Tarrantino flick or read 50 Shades Of Grey but OMG do the binge deeply upon unforgiveness and bitterness towards anyone who has slighted them.

Yep, if you offend them then you are *persona non grata* for the rest of your life.

I remember one time I was at a BBQ back in 2004 and this lady asked me what I thought of Kirk Cameron's Left Behind movie. To wit I said, 'Left behind? Is that the movie where a crack whore gets her right butt cheek blown off in a drug deal gone awry and from then on they nicknamed her, 'Old Left Behind?'

Fast forward ten years later to 2014 when I once again bumped into the same lady who was still PO'ed at me for my Left Behind joke. She said she had been bitter against me for over a decade just because I dissed Cameron's cheesy and erroneous escalatological flick.

When she told me of her offense, I could see that she was still stewing in her juices. So I apologized for my childish, but really funny joke about a bad movie, and then I told her she needed to get a life because she was getting bent out of shape for a truly inconsequential reason which probably sent her reeling into another decade of bitterness and offense.

In Matthew 18, Jesus discusses stumbling blocks and brothers sinning against each other and how to lovingly correct one another when we do transgress our bros.

Peter, feeling a little extra, extra spiritual, pipes up and says, "Lord, how often shall my brother sin against me and I forgive him? Up to seven times?" Jesus said to him, "I do not say to you, up to seven times, but up to seventy times seven."

Peter, I'm sure, thought that forgiving a brother seven times was serious spiritual stuff but Jesus was like, 'Dude ... you' ain't even close. Try timesing that by seventy.'

Yep, if our brother wrongs us 490 times we are to forgive him.

Some ragers, who live off bitterness, are probably thinking, 'Okay. I'll forgive someone 490 times, but to hell with them on the 491st offense.' Which is completely missing the lesson clearly taught here by Jesus, namely, forgiveness should be free flowing and never-ending. Why? Well, that's how God deals with His elect's foibles, that's why.

Face it folks, we're goofy sintards.

We both think and do the abominable, day in and day out.

We commit sins of commission and sins of omission on a regular basis.

Albeit, true Christians are free from the power and penalty of sin, we, unfortunately, do sin and are in constant need of the forgiveness afforded to us by Christ's sacrifice, mercy and grace.

We need it.

We want it.

We must have it.

What's weird is that as much as we're in need of it and thankful for it we don't extend it to others when they bump into us and sin against us.

We're like, 'God have mercy on me and then when some-one sins against us we're like, Lord, kill that son-of-a-b****!'

Jesus jackhammers that jaundiced spirit.

Jesus' message is, If you have received forgiveness then your only recourse is to give forgiveness or He calls you, 'a wicked slave' and in 'anger' The Father 'hands' the unforgiv-ing person 'over to the torturers'. And that my friends does not sound good at all, does it?

So, how does this forgiveness motif tie into Jesus exhibiting masculinity?

Well, to me, it takes a big boy to let things go.

It takes a mature person to realize we all need forgiveness and, therefore, who are we to not give it to others?

It's only the petty and fragile little egos who won't pay forward the forgiveness and grace that they received.

Chapter 27

Marriage & Divorce Matthew 19:1-9

---

1 When Jesus had finished these words, He departed
from Galilee and came into the region of Judea beyond
the Jordan; 2 and large crowds followed Him, and He
healed them there.

3 Some Pharisees came to Jesus, testing Him and ask-
ing, "Is it lawful for a man to divorce his wife for any
reason at all?" 4 And He answered and said, "Have
you not read that He who created them from the begin-
ning made them male and female, 5 and said, 'For this
reason a man shall leave his father and mother and be
joined to his wife, and the two shall become one flesh'?
6 So they are no longer two, but one flesh. What there-
fore God has joined together, let no man separate." 7
*They *said to Him, "Why then did Moses command to*
give her a certificate of divorce and send her away?" 8
*He *said to them, "Because of your hardness of heart*
Moses permitted you to divorce your wives; but from
the beginning it has not been this way. 9 And I say to
you, whoever divorces his wife, except for immorality,

and marries another woman commits adultery."

Matthew 19:1-9 (NASB)

This chapter is going to get me in hot water.

Yep, I'm bracing for the hate mail now.

All I have to say is, 'I'm just the messenger. Take it up with Jesus if you don't like it. He said it. Not me.'

If a minister preaches what Jesus preached about divorce in our no-fault, fifty percent of all marriages fail, milieu he had better have some Christ-like brass *cojones*.

When the religious dorks tried to trick Jesus into besmirching Himself with an insidious question regarding divorce, Jesus did what He always does when He's talking to devils, He quoted the word of God back to them (Genesis 2:24).

In Matthew 19 Jesus makes it clear that marriage is ordained of God and that the man and the wife are to be one until one of them takes the big dirt nap.

Please note: He said that marriage is between a male and a female. Not a male and a male. Or a female and a female. Or a Trans person and a non-Trans person. Or a Trans person and another Trans person.

He clearly says that what God joins together and calls a marriage, of which is not to be separated, is between a biological dude and a dudette. Period.

A cyclops can see what Jesus' teaching on divorce is: namely, He restricted divorces except for adultery and He disallowed remarriage of those who did divorce unrighteously, calling their remarriage an adulterous act if they remarry (Matthew 5:32; Matthew 19:9).

Yikes, eh?

Again, don't hate me. He said it. I'm just repeating what He preached.

In Jesus' day the rabbis had taken the Law of Moses and had twisted it to permit divorce for pretty much any stupid and selfish reason.

Jesus crushed those notions with His stringent opposition to divorce.

Jesus taught the only time you are free to leave who you are married to, if you wish, is if they cheated on you with another person.

Paul, in his first letter to the Corinthians yields up another reason for dumping your mate. Check it out …

'Yet if the unbelieving one leaves, let him leave; the brother or the sister is not under bondage in such cases, but God has called us to peace.' - 1Corinthians 7:15

In other words, if the non-Christian spouse abandons the Christian spouse, the believer is under no obligation to stay in that marriage.

So, what we have here children are two pretty specific

reasons allowed for by God for divorce: 1). adultery and 2). abandonment.

Lastly, is divorce the unpardonable sin?

Of course not.

But God does hate it (Malachi 2:16).

Even though He himself is a divorcee (Jeremiah 3:8).

I know one thing for certain after meditating on Matthew 19:1-9, Jesus takes marriage and divorce way more seriously than most 21st century Christians do.

Chapter 28

True Greatness
Matthew 20:17-28

---

17 As Jesus was about to go up to Jerusalem, He took
the twelve disciples aside by themselves, and on the
way He said to them, 18 "Behold, we are going up to
Jerusalem; and the Son of Man will be delivered to the
chief priests and scribes, and they will condemn Him
to death, 19 and will hand Him over to the Gentiles to
mock and scourge and crucify Him, and on the third
day He will be raised up."

20 Then the mother of the sons of Zebedee came to Jesus with her sons, bowing down and making a request
of Him. 21 And He said to her, "What do you wish?"
She *said to Him, "Command that in Your kingdom
these two sons of mine may sit one on Your right and
one on Your left." 22 But Jesus answered, "You do not
know what you are asking. Are you able to drink the cup
that I am about to drink?" They *said to Him, "We are
able." 23 He *said to them, "My cup you shall drink;
but to sit on My right and on My left, this is not Mine to
give, but it is for those for whom it has been prepared
by My Father."

24 And hearing this, the ten became indignant with the two brothers. 25 But Jesus called them to Himself and said, "You know that the rulers of the Gentiles lord it over them, and their great men exercise authority over them. 26 It is not this way among you, but whoever wishes to become great among you shall be your servant, 27 and whoever wishes to be first among you shall be your slave; 28 just as the Son of Man did not come to be served, but to serve, and to give His life a ransom for many."

Matthew 20:17-28 (NASB)

It's amazing how daft Jesus' original disciples were.

The original Terrific Twelve did not 'get Him' even though they were privileged to hear and see the most epic Man and events to ever to occur in world history, i.e. Christ's person and His works.

Indeed, they had front row seats to the greatest individual to ever to schlep this *terra firma*.

They had Him personally teach them the mysteries of the Kingdom of God.

They watched Him cast out demons, heal the sick and raise the dead.

They watched Him walk on water and rebuke thunderstorms.

They watched Him harshly jetblast arrogant religious leaders and speak life into lowly sinful commoners.

They watched Him fashion a whip and clear the religious

punks from The Temple.

They watched Him turn tap water into top shelf wine.

They watched The Holy One humbly serve unholy ones.

And in this passage, they just heard Him clearly say that He's going forth to be condemned to death; mocked, scourged, and crucified by the Gentiles.

Yep, the disciples' Lord and Savior and best buddy just unloaded on them, again, that His death is imminent and the only thing on the disciples' mind is who's the greatest among them and who gets to sit closest to Jesus?

That, my beloved, is what is called, 'weird.'

Wouldn't you think it weird if you told your men's group at church that you're going to be cruelly martyred tomorrow and their main concern is what glamor photo they should use for their Instagram profile pic?

These preening peacocks are talking about titles, positions, power and pride.

They still haven't learned a thing.

The disciples, at this juncture, want to be exalted.

They want to be ogled.

They want a power position.

They want to be the Christian glory boy on social media and at Christian conferences.

James and John even got their mommy involved to lean on Jesus in order to secure their place of pre-eminence in His coming kingdom.

Unreal.

Does that not shock you? That after three years of intensive basic-training, by The Son of Man Himself, they're still full of themselves and are seeking personal exaltation from a Savior who, 'made Himself of no reputation, and took upon Him the form of a servant, and was made in the likeness of men: And being found in fashion as a man, He humbled Himself, and became obedient unto death, even the death of the cross' (Philippians 2:7,8)

It floors me how dense the disciples were.

It also floors me how dense His 21st century disciples still are and I'll put myself at the head of the line for that insult.

That said, the disciples' prideful and selfish blunders highlighted here in Matthew 20 also encourages me because, I too, can be one self-obsessed hideous Christian and if He still accepted, used and straightened out His first-century handpicked boys then, hopefully, He'll do the same for my stupid backside.

So, what happened to James and John?

Did they cease to be the 'Look at me! I'm Sandra Dee' type of Christian?

You bet they did.

They learned a big lesson that the Kingdom of God wasn't about them, but Him and that lesson came in a big way once the Holy Ghost was poured out on 'em in the upper room. From that point onward, you don't hear them saying the same goofy crap they said prior to His crucifixion and the outpouring of the Holy Spirit.

Indeed, they selflessly and sacrificially 'drank the cup' of suffering that Christ promised them they would drink.

James was the first martyr in the scripture. He was beheaded for his bold witness of the Gospel in AD 44.

John, after establishing many churches, was banished to the Isle of Patmos.

Both ceased and desisted talking about themselves and gloried only in Christ and Christ alone.

May God free us from our effeminate self-obsession with fake 'greatness' that comes with pride and titles and make us truly great in God's eyes with a selfless, servant, Christ-like spirit.

Chapter 29

Outrageous Jesus
Matthew 21:12-17

---

12 And Jesus entered the temple and drove out all those who were buying and selling in the temple, and overturned the tables of the money changers and the seats of those who were selling doves. 13 And He *said to them, "It is written, 'My house shall be called a house of prayer'; but you are making it a robbers' den."

14 And the blind and the lame came to Him in the temple, and He healed them. 15 But when the chief priests and the scribes saw the wonderful things that He had done, and the children who were shouting in the temple, "Hosanna to the Son of David," they became indignant 16 and said to Him, "Do You hear what these children are saying?" And Jesus *said to them, "Yes; have you never read, 'Out of the mouth of infants and nursing babies You have prepared praise for Yourself'?" 17 And He left them and went out of the city to Bethany, and spent the night there.

Matthew 21:12-17 (NASB)

Dang, man.

Jesus got angry, eh?

Like in real angry.

As in, bounce-scallywags-out-of-the-temple-and-flip-over tables-and-chairs, angry.

He was ticked, I'm telling you.

What's weird is, the day before was very positive and very upbeat. You'd think Jesus would still be basking in the glow of a great day. Check it out …

> *1 When they had approached Jerusalem and had come*
> *to Bethphage, at the Mount of Olives, then Jesus sent*
> *two disciples, 2 saying to them, "Go into the village op-*
> *posite you, and immediately you will find a donkey tied*
> *there and a colt with her; untie them and bring them*
> *to Me. 3 If anyone says anything to you, you shall say,*
> *'The Lord has need of them,' and immediately he will*
> *send them." 4 This took place to fulfill what was spoken*
> *through the prophet:*
>
> *5 "Say to the daughter of Zion,*
>
> *'Behold your King is coming to you,*
>
> *Gentle, and mounted on a donkey,*
>
> *Even on a colt, the foal of a beast of burden.'"*
>
> *6 The disciples went and did just as Jesus had instruct-*
> *ed them, 7 and brought the donkey and the colt, and*
> *laid their coats on them; and He sat on the coats. 8*
> *Most of the crowd spread their coats in the road, and*
> *others were cutting branches from the trees and spread-*
> *ing them in the road. 9 The crowds going ahead of Him,*

and those who followed, were shouting,

"Hosanna to the Son of David;

Blessed is He who comes in the name of the Lord;

Hosanna in the highest!"

10 When He had entered Jerusalem, all the city was stirred, saying, "Who is this?" 11 And the crowds were saying, "This is the prophet Jesus, from Nazareth in Galilee."

Matthew 21:1-11 (NASB)

Matthew 21:1-11 is what theologians call, 'Christ's Triumphal Entry' into Jerusalem.

What would seem like a mundane religious event in our postmodern secular context, that's bereft of any biblical background, this act by Jesus is loaded with prophetic significance.

Aside from all the attesting miracles and works Jesus performed in His three-year earthly ministry, Jesus chooses to make another fulfillment of prophecy unmistakable, as His incarnate work on earth comes to close.

In the aforementioned account, Jesus is stating that He is The One who was prophesied to come in Zechariah 9:9 (NASB).

Rejoice greatly, O daughter of Zion!

Shout in triumph, O daughter of Jerusalem!

Behold, your king is coming to you;

He is just and endowed with salvation,

Humble, and mounted on a donkey,

Even on a colt, the foal of a donkey.

The Triumphal Entry was clearly a symbolic act and every serious Jew knew the weight of the way Jesus entered Jerusalem equated another earthly game changer.

To those who longed for the Messiah ... well … their day had come.

Here He is and they were happy about it!

They were stoked.

The Triumphal Entry was exactly that: a very positive and electric event, in our parlance.

The King had come, endowed with salvation, humble and riding a donkey and the city was lit because of it.

Those who weren't up to scratch with biblical symbolism were wondering, 'What's all the ruckus about?'

Those somewhat in the know told the inquisitive dullards, 'This is the *prophet* Jesus, from Nazareth in Galilee.'

Let's recap, shall we?

Again, from a *prima facie* standpoint, Matthew 21:1-11 is a pretty chipper day.

Most of the folks were happy.

Jesus was happy.

Heck, what could go wrong?

What could go wrong, and did go wrong, was Jesus cannot turn the prophet off in Him and the next day, when He entered the Temple and He saw it turned into a Christian Booksellers Association filled with greasy hucksters selling religious crap to gullible googins, the gentle donkey rider morphed into a PO'ed prophet.

And that's where Jesus differs greatly from most ministers.

Most ministers today, if they would have seen the creeps selling in the Temple back in Jesus' day, probably would have thought ...

- 'Hey, why didn't I think of that? What a great way to make money and serve God.'
- 'Y'know, we should set up a meeting with these merchants to sell our sappy devotionals here next Sabbath!'
- 'Let's take some selfies with the hot rabbis so we can name drop at the next Hosanna Conference.'
- 'Sure it seems tacky, but I hear 1% of the proceeds go to trying to rescue Hassidic Jewish teenagers addicted to Samaritan rap music and smoking the Devil's lettuce.'

When Jesus got an eye-full of how the Temple had been turned into a hangout for hoodlums, He tossed the joint.

Like in violently ransacking the place.

Jesus made zero excuses for this crass marketing in an environment designated for prayer.

So Jesus made certain, that prior to His exit from this planet, people understood, loud and clear, that He hates this type of tawdry behavior in His Father's House.

Please note: He could have ignored the situation in the Temple. Y'know … pretend it wasn't there and it wasn't odious.

Also, He could have just prayed that God would open their eyes to see the error of their greedy ways.

In addition, He could have told Bartholemew to blog about how bad it was for the historical record.

But instead Jesus' 'toxic masculinity' got the best of Him and He threw the bastards out of His Dad's digs and you know who loved that?

Young people.

You know who hated Jesus' outrageous behavior?

The religious leaders.

Yep, young people thought Jesus whuppin' some rank religious backside was so awesome they were running around the Temple singing His praises.

The religious leaders, however, eh … not so much. They were more offended by the righteous and rowdy rebel youth who dug what Jesus had just done more than they were by the thieves selling in the Temple.

Finally, next time some church lady queries during Bible Study, 'What Would Jesus Do?' Tell her it depends. Sometimes He shows compassion and sometimes He kicks some ass.

Chapter 30

Few Are Chosen
Matthew 22:1-14

---

*1 Jesus spoke to them again in parables, saying, 2 "The
kingdom of heaven may be compared to a king who
gave a wedding feast for his son. 3 And he sent out his
slaves to call those who had been invited to the wedding feast, and they were unwilling to come. 4 Again he
sent out other slaves saying, 'Tell those who have been
invited, "Behold, I have prepared my dinner; my oxen
and my fattened livestock are all butchered and everything is ready; come to the wedding feast."' 5 But they
paid no attention and went their way, one to his own
farm, another to his business, 6 and the rest seized his
slaves and mistreated them and killed them. 7 But the
king was enraged, and he sent his armies and destroyed
those murderers and set their city on fire. 8 Then he
*said to his slaves, 'The wedding is ready, but those
who were invited were not worthy. 9 Go therefore to the
main highways, and as many as you find there, invite
to the wedding feast.' 10 Those slaves went out into the
streets and gathered together all they found, both evil
and good; and the wedding hall was filled with dinner*

guests.

*11 "But when the king came in to look over the dinner guests, he saw a man there who was not dressed in wedding clothes, 12 and he *said to him, 'Friend, how did you come in here without wedding clothes?' And the man was speechless. 13 Then the king said to the servants, 'Bind him hand and foot, and throw him into the outer darkness; in that place there will be weeping and gnashing of teeth.' 14 For many are called, but few are chosen."*

Matthew 22:1-14 (NASB)

This is a terrifying parable.

Most, if not all of Jesus' parables, have some type of holy gloom to them which makes many PC pastors avoid teaching them like Meghan Markle shuns a Piers Morgan interview request.

This parable has doom and gloom in abundance.

Jesus' maledictions, in this fresh story from Matthew, are aimed right at the self-righteous that have rejected His gracious message He's been offering them for the last three years and are now on the verge of having Him murdered.

Yep, this is the final week of His natural life.

Soon, Jesus will be crucified and He's well aware of what's coming.

Ergo, in case people misunderstood His messages for the last 36 months and thought they were okie dokie because of their external religious adherence to the traditions of men,

Christ makes it real plain in this parable that they are doomed and they will be replaced by another people who accept His invitation to the 'Wedding Feast.'

In Matthew 22:1-14, we see Christ 'shaking the dust off His feet' to His obstreperous Jewish foes who have rejected Him and The Gospel and He does it with a story about a big party.

Let's unpack it, shall we?

The 'King' character in this tale is, God The Father.

The 'Son' character is Jesus The Son.

The 'slaves' are the New Testament preachers of the Gospel.

The 'invited' are the Jews who rejected Jesus.

The 'Wedding Feast' is the call to salvation, in Christ alone.

Check it out.

Jesus likens the kingdom of heaven … or salvation … to an epic wedding party thrown by a king.

Please note: He didn't liken salvation to …

1. A grueling list of do's and don'ts. Or ...
2. Listening to some dopey kid's first clarinet recital. Or ...
3. Watching paint dry. Or …
4. French kissing your sister. Or …

5. Anything miserable that one would loathe to watch or do.

Indeed, Jesus, the Master storyteller, compares the call to salvation by faith in Him and His finished work alone to getting an invitation to a grand event.

When a powerful person throws a party it ain't like those haggard parties we had in High School where we ate chicken gizzards and got wasted on Mickey Big Mouths and then watched Rhonda do a topless drunk table dance on a rickety picnic table until she passed out in her vomit.

Rich and powerful peeps love to be lavish when they roll out the red carpet for their guests. There's champagne, caviar, beautiful people, excellent music, wonderful decorations and if you're in Texas … epic BBQ, of course.

In other words, folks … this party doesn't suck.

Anyone with a lick of sense would want to attend such a feast, right?

In this parable, the king sends forth the call to the 'invited' that it is go time … the party is officially on.

And what's the invited guest's response?

Well, one group blew off attending the epic party and obsessed on worldly interests instead and another group actually mistreated and killed the messengers who were announcing this grand shindig.

So, what did the King do?

Well, little kiddies, the King got ticked and sent his troops to slaughter the murderers and torch the town, that's 'What'.

Sounds kind of like what happened to Jerusalem in 70AD, eh?

Anyway … once it was made clear the 'called' weren't coming, the King switches gears and opens up the party to whomever, both good and evil, because His Son will have a well deserved full house.

Now the party is packed and you'd figure the King would be cool, but alas, He ain't. The King spots a dude who's not donned in wedding attire and immediately has this cat hogtied and tossed into a miserable abyss.

And that my friends, makes this story hopeful and terrifying.

It's terrifying for those who blow off God's call to salvation because they're too wrapped up in their own pursuits.

It's terrifying for those who, because of their religious traditions, attack Jesus and His messengers' message.

It's terrifying if you assume you're an okay partygoer but you're not clothed in Christ's robe of imputed righteousness but are instead clothed in your own religious works (Isaiah 61:10, Job 29:14, Revelation 19:8, Isaiah 59:17, Zechariah 3:4, Revelation 3:4, 2Corinthians 5:21, Rom.4:22-25).

It's incredibly hopeful, especially for 'evil' people, in that they too get invited to the party and enjoy the King's bounty as long as they're properly clothed in the Son's 'wedding clothes'.

The mealy-mouthed *faux* Christ of the American church's machinations would never be so stringent on who does and doesn't get to sit at the wedding table, but the real Jesus was and is.

It takes holy *cojones* to preach 'many are called, but few are chosen.'

And that's why Jesus is so appealing and politically correct pastors are so appalling.

Chapter 31

Eight Woes
Matthew 23:13-36

---

13 "But woe to you, scribes and Pharisees, hypocrites,
because you shut off the kingdom of heaven from peo-
ple; for you do not enter in yourselves, nor do you allow
those who are entering to go in. 14 [Woe to you, scribes
and Pharisees, hypocrites, because you devour wid-
ows' houses, and for a pretense you make long prayers;
therefore you will receive greater condemnation.]

15 "Woe to you, scribes and Pharisees, hypocrites, be-
cause you travel around on sea and land to make one
proselyte; and when he becomes one, you make him
twice as much a son of hell as yourselves.

16 "Woe to you, blind guides, who say, 'Whoever
swears by the temple, that is nothing; but whoever
swears by the gold of the temple is obligated.' 17 You
fools and blind men! Which is more important, the gold
or the temple that sanctified the gold? 18 And, 'Who-
ever swears by the altar, that is nothing, but whoever
swears by the offering on it, he is obligated.' 19 You
blind men, which is more important, the offering, or the

*altar that sanctifies the offering? 20 Therefore, whoev-
er swears by the altar, swears both by the altar and by
everything on it. 21 And whoever swears by the temple,
swears both by the temple and by Him who dwells within it. 22 And whoever swears by heaven, swears both by
the throne of God and by Him who sits upon it.*

*23 "Woe to you, scribes and Pharisees, hypocrites! For
you tithe mint and dill and cummin, and have neglected
the weightier provisions of the law: justice and mercy
and faithfulness; but these are the things you should
have done without neglecting the others. 24 You blind
guides, who strain out a gnat and swallow a camel!*

*25 "Woe to you, scribes and Pharisees, hypocrites! For
you clean the outside of the cup and of the dish, but
inside they are full of robbery and self-indulgence. 26
You blind Pharisee, first clean the inside of the cup and
of the dish, so that the outside of it may become clean
also.*

*27 "Woe to you, scribes and Pharisees, hypocrites! For
you are like whitewashed tombs which on the outside
appear beautiful, but inside they are full of dead men's
bones and all uncleanness. 28 So you, too, outwardly
appear righteous to men, but inwardly you are full of
hypocrisy and lawlessness.*

*29 "Woe to you, scribes and Pharisees, hypocrites! For
you build the tombs of the prophets and adorn the mon-
uments of the righteous, 30 and say, 'If we had been
living in the days of our fathers, we would not have
been partners with them in shedding the blood of the
prophets.' 31 So you testify against yourselves, that you
are sons of those who murdered the prophets. 32 Fill
up, then, the measure of the guilt of your fathers. 33 You
serpents, you brood of vipers, how will you escape the
sentence of hell?*

34 "Therefore, behold, I am sending you prophets and

> *wise men and scribes; some of them you will kill and crucify, and some of them you will scourge in your synagogues, and persecute from city to city, 35 so that upon you may fall the guilt of all the righteous blood shed on earth, from the blood of righteous Abel to the blood of Zechariah, the son of Berechiah, whom you murdered between the temple and the altar. 36 Truly I say to you, all these things will come upon this generation.*
>
> Matthew 23:13-36 (NASB)

Well, after plowing through that royal rebuke given by The Prince of Peace one thing is for certain: Jesus is not fond of religious hogwash or those who sling it.

If you're in the God business for money, or power, or to propagate your self-righteous religious traditions to poor unwashed rubes looking to connect with heaven, then you are eternally screwed according to the Wonderful Counselor.

Jesus made certain the religious and self-preening hoity-toity crowd got that message loud and clear with His very last public sermon.

Yep, folks this was His last public podcast.

Last words are interesting.

Last words can be emotional, hilarious, inspirational and flatout freaky.

For instance, check out these last words from famous people taken from the book, Last Words of Notable People ...

George Orwell's last written words were, "At fifty, everyone has the face he deserves."

Elvis Presley's last words were, "I'm going to the bathroom to read."

Frank Sinatra died after saying, "I'm losing it."

When Harriet Tubman was dying she gathered her family and sang together. Her last words were, "Swing low, sweet chariot."

Composer Jean-Philippe Rameau blasted a priest who tried to sing to him while he was dying saying, "What the devil do you mean to sing to me, priest? You are out of tune."

Leonardo da Vinci's last words were, "I have offended God and mankind because my work did not reach the quality it should have."

Louise-Marie-Thérèse de Saint Maurice, Comtesse de Vercellis farted as she was dying and she said, "Good. A woman who can fart is not dead."

Murderer James W. Rodgers was put in front of a firing squad in Utah and asked if he had a last request. He replied, "Bring me a bullet-proof vest."

John Wayne died at age 72. His last words went to his wife. He said, "Of course I know who you are. You're my girl. I love you."

Sir Winston Churchill's last words were, "I'm bored with it all."

Bo Diddley died giving a thumbs-up as he listened to the song "Walk Around Heaven." His last word was "Wow."

And according to Steve Jobs' sister, the Apple founder's last words were, "Oh wow. Oh wow. Oh wow."

My dad's last words he uttered as he was passing away were, " Jesus, Jesus, Jesus."

Now granted the rebuke Jesus laid on the Pharisees weren't His last last words. His last words, "Father, into your hands I commit My spirit (Luke 23:46)", were uttered from the cross but this was His last public sermon and it was anything but sweet and amorphous.

If most ministers in today's sassy Catholic or Protestant churches were given one last message to preach, I'm willing to guess it wouldn't be a thunderstruck, public rebuke, holy jetblast to false teachers.

Please note: Jesus' last message wasn't about love. It wasn't about unity. It wasn't about tolerance. It wasn't against hunting or eating meat. It wasn't about peace. It wasn't about heaven and the sweet by and by. It had no kumbaya in it. It was a curse, a malediction, upon the heralds of a works based self-righteous religion preached by the religious leaders of His day.

His last public message was, 'Woe'.

'Woe' is a biblical word that doesn't get too much play in our vocab nowadays.

If you got a 'woe' shot at you, your church, city, state or nation it meant that you were in deep deep doo-doo according to the word of God.

For the uninitiated, 'Woe', biblically speaking, was an exclamation of divine judgment leveled at God's foes.

Woe's were given to:

God's enemies. Isaiah 33:1; Jeremiah 48:1-2; Nahum 3:1-7; Habakkuk 2:6-20; Zephaniah 2:5

God's faithless people. Hos. 7:13-16; Isaiah 30:1-2; Isaiah 45:9-10; Jeremiah . 4:13-18; Ezekiel 16:23-27

Shoddy shepherds of God's people. Jeremiah 23:1-2; Ezekiel 13:1-9; Ezekiel 34:1-10; Zephaniah3:1-4; Zechariah 11:15-17

Those who are complacent in their suburbia religion. Amos 6:1-7; Amos 5:18-24

Those who neglected the downtrodden. Isaiah 10:1-4; Isaiah 5:8-23; Jeremiah 22:13-19; Micah 2:1-3

A godless world that blows off Jesus. Revelation 8:13; Revelation 12:12; Revelation 18:10,16-17,19

Those who are addicted to comfort and love having everyone like them. Luke 6:24-26

Those whose religion blinds themselves and misleads others. Luke 11:52; Matthew 23:13-33; Luke 11:42-51

Those who cause others to sin. Matthew 18:7; Luke 17:1-3

Those who betray the Son of Man. Matthew 26:24; Mark 14:21; Luke 22:22

* FYI: The word translated 'how dreadful' in the scripture is the same word that elsewhere is translated "woe".

Yep, Jesus wielded a 'Woe Sermon' at false teachers for His public finale.

Here's eight specific reasons the Savior damned them in His last sermon and encouraged His followers to do the opposite of what these clowns do.

1. Their lives were roadblocks to God's kingdom. They refuse to enter, and wouldn't let anyone else in either.
2. They took advantage of widows and their wealth with their long fake prayers.
3. They went halfway around the world to make a convert, but once they got one they turned into a replica of themselves making him twice the son of hell, double-damned.
4. They played religious word games that gave them a supposed loophole to lie and deceive people and still be considered 'godly'.
5. They nitpicked over the cosmically inconsequential while blowing off the major issues of God such as justice and mercy and faithfulness.
6. They focused on bolstering up an appearance of godliness but inwardly they were full of the maggots of greed and gluttony.

7. They loved being looked at as well-manicured, well-healed, religious dainties but in Jesus's eyes they were total frauds.
8. They praised the prophets of the past but in reality, if they would've been there during the various prophets' ministry, they would've been the ones who would've killed them.

Once again, it takes *cojones* to live and preach such a message and Christ had them in spades.

Do you?

Chapter 32

Many False Prophets Matthew 24:11

11 Many false prophets will arise and will mislead many.

Matthew 24:11 (NASB)

Matthew 24 has spawned more speculation than Linda McCartney's 1990 'Hey Jude' isolated vocal track did regarding whether or not she could actually sing.

I have my views regarding what Jesus is talking about in this epic apocalyptic chapter and you have yours and to each his own.

This chapter definitely provides great late night fodder for chummy conversations and debates about the 'end of all things'. Especially between Reformed Presbyterians and Southern Baptists. Good Lawd!

Personally, I believe Jesus was talking about the destruction of Jerusalem in 70AD and not the COVID-19 virus of 2020 but that's a topic for another book, eh?

This slim tome's focus is on the overt masculine traits of Jesus and the one I'd like to highlight in this chapter, that isn't fuzzy at all, is Him warning His boys about false prophets. Yep, Jesus gave zero foxtrots about the dealers of deception and their feelings and thus, He whipped them at every turn and at every post.

For example, Jesus' first sermon for His *amigos* and the masses (Matthew 7:15) warned of false prophets.

In His last sermon, Jesus barbecued the false prophets (Matthew 23:13-36) eternally condemning them to an everlasting hell.

In between His first and last sermons, He drop-kicked them every chance He got both in private and in public.

Now, in His final personal powwow with His disciples He warned them three times in two verses to not be taken in by religious furphy spewers (Matthew 24:11, 24).

It's clear to this old redneck that Jesus cares about truth and He has no problem exposing hacks who torture the scripture and deceive undiscerning dippy people.

Speaking of truth, the Church in America ain't got time for truth. They want to have their ears tickled and their gelatinous belly stroked with soothing messages from mellow and charming voices that tell them 'they're just fine' when in reality they're probably going to split hell wide open upon expiration.

Sound doctrine isn't hip any longer to the-make-it-up-as-you-go-Christian.

You could probably fit all the folks in the U.S.A., who actually care about apologetics, systematic theology and the Solas of The Reformation into a small church's broom closet. I have actually heard 'Christians' emphatically state that, 'they don't care what the Bible says'.

It's really sad that most ministers, let alone the general masses, don't know what The Westminster Shorter Catechism is but they're punchdrunk on Hillsong and Bethel tunes, their church's man-made traditions and/or the ubiquitous Be A Better You bevy of banal books.

So, for those who still care, and do not want to be deceived and damned, here's how one spots a false prophet.

I've gleaned and paraphrased these six traits from the Puritan great, Thomas Brooks.

Number One. False prophets are people pleasers. They'll tell whomever whatever for power, profit, praise, and approval. They preach to tickle your ear and not bring you to repentance and a true knowledge of a Holy God. The disturbing thing is there's a whole lot of folks in Christendom that want to be lied to. Check out these horrifying scriptures.

> *31 The prophets prophesy falsely, And the priests rule on their own authority; And My people love it so! But what will you do at the end of it?*
>
> Jeremiah 5:31 (NASB)

9 For this is a rebellious people, false sons, Sons who refuse to listen To the instruction of the Lord; 10 Who say to the seers, "You must not see visions"; And to the prophets, "You must not prophesy to us what is right, Speak to us pleasant words, Prophesy illusions. 11 "Get out of the way, turn aside from the path, Let us hear no more about the Holy One of Israel."

Isaiah 30:9-11 (NASB)

I solemnly charge you in the presence of God and of Christ Jesus, who is to judge the living and the dead, and by His appearing and His kingdom: 2 preach the word; be ready in season and out of season; reprove, rebuke, exhort, with great patience and instruction. 3 For the time will come when they will not endure sound doctrine; but wanting to have their ears tickled, they will accumulate for themselves teachers in accordance to their own desires, 4 and will turn away their ears from the truth and will turn aside to myths.

2Timothy 4:1-4 (NASB)

11 For this reason God will send upon them a deluding influence so that they will believe what is false, 12 in order that they all may be judged who did not believe the truth, but took pleasure in wickedness.

2Thessalonians.2:11-12 (NASB)

These buttkissers are good.

Real good.

They'll fluff your pillows ... pour you a coffee … and plunge you right into the abyss with their lies.

Yep, they'll charm you with their dally and their wit but they are bereft of the fear of God and holy dread and will undo your soul if you buy their crack. The smooth talking religious yapper is a soul poisoner. Run from them. Get around pastors who'll preach the truth even if it grates your flesh.

Number Two. False prophets despise true ministers of the Gospel.

This fear and loathing has been going on since the dawn of time. False prophets, who're full of lies, hype and spin, hate and I mean hate, those who hold tight to *sola scriptura.*

Check it out: these false prophets will fling dirt, gossip, write anonymous and disparaging blogs; go hashtag crazy on Facebook trying to ruin and sully the name of those who faithfully carry out the Master's task of preaching the Apostles' doctrine.

Paul was constantly attacked by false brethren. They mocked his message, spread lies about him, beat him to a pulp several times, and even ridiculed his appearance (2Corinthians 10:10).

Why? Well, he was kicking their lying backside with this thing called, 'the truth', so they had to take him down someway.

Here's a FYI: If you're around a 'Christian' and all they do is talk mad smack about a serious saint who greatly esteems the word of God then you're probably in proximity to a false prophet or one in the making.

Number Three. They declare that which comes from their own whirring tin-brain and not the balance of the scripture.

Oh to be certain, it's couched in very religious verbiage and traditions but it's not biblical.

> *14 Then the Lord said to me, "The prophets are prophesying falsehood in My name. I have neither sent them nor commanded them nor spoken to them; they are prophesying to you a false vision, divination, futility and the deception of their own minds.*
>
> Jeremiah 14:14 (NASB)

> *Thus says the Lord of hosts, "Do not listen to the words of the prophets who are prophesying to you. They are leading you into futility; They speak a vision of their own imagination, Not from the mouth of the Lord. "They keep saying to those who despise Me, 'The Lord has said, "You will have peace"'; And as for everyone who walks in the stubbornness of his own heart, They say, 'Calamity will not come upon you.' ... 21 "I did not send these prophets, But they ran. I did not speak to them, But they prophesied. "But if they had stood in My council, Then they would have announced My words to My people, And would have turned them back from their evil way And from the evil of their deeds.*
>
> Jeremiah 23:16-17;21,22 (NASB)

> *20 To the law and to the testimony! If they do not speak according to this word, it is because they have no dawn.*
>
> Isaiah 8:20 (NASB)

So, before you deep dive into some religious system, or start following some particular leader, run what they're selling thoroughly through the gauntlet of the scripture and then run it through again. Be like the Bereans mentioned here in the book of Acts who examined the scriptures daily to see whether what Paul and Silas taught was legit …

10 The brethren immediately sent Paul and Silas away
by night to Berea, and when they arrived, they went
into the synagogue of the Jews. 11 Now these were more
noble-minded than those in Thessalonica, for they re-
ceived the word with great eagerness, examining the
Scriptures daily to see whether these things were so. 12
Therefore many of them believed, along with a number
of prominent Greek women and men.

Acts 17:10-12 (NASB)

Number Four. False prophets obsess over minutiae and blow off the truly great and weighty things of God and that which is a direct benefit to the souls' of men.

3 As I urged you upon my departure for Macedonia,
remain on at Ephesus so that you may instruct certain
men not to teach strange doctrines, 4 nor to pay atten-
tion to myths and endless genealogies, which give rise
to mere speculation rather than furthering the admin-
istration of God which is by faith. 5 But the goal of our
instruction is love from a pure heart and a good con-
science and a sincere faith. 6 For some men, straying
from these things, have turned aside to fruitless discus-
sion, 7 wanting to be teachers of the Law, even though
they do not understand either what they are saying or
the matters about which they make confident assertions.

1Timothy 1:3-7 (NASB)

23 "Woe to you, scribes and Pharisees, hypocrites! For
you tithe mint and dill and cummin, and have neglected
the weightier provisions of the law: justice and mercy
and faithfulness; but these are the things you should
have done without neglecting the others. 24 You blind
guides, who strain out a gnat and swallow a camel!

Matthew 23:23-24 (NASB)

3 If anyone advocates a different doctrine and does

not agree with sound words, those of our Lord Jesus Christ, and with the doctrine conforming to godliness,
4 he is conceited and understands nothing; but he has a morbid interest in controversial questions and disputes about words, out of which arise envy, strife, abusive language, evil suspicions,
5 and constant friction between men of depraved mind and deprived of the truth, who suppose that godliness is a means of gain.

1Timothy 6.3-5 (NASB)

Number Five. False prophets seek to win men over to their opinions and not to the person and work of Christ. Jesus put it this way …

15 "Woe to you, scribes and Pharisees, hypocrites, because you travel around on sea and land to make one proselyte; and when he becomes one, you make him twice as much a son of hell as yourselves.

Matthew 23:15 (NASB)

The false teachers in Jesus' day didn't give one flying flibbertigibbet whether a person truly knew God or not. What they were interested in is making fresh stooges for their religious machine.

Number Six. False prophets look at congregants as cold hard cash and not souls that they're responsible for.

1 But false prophets also arose among the people, just as there will also be false teachers among you, who will secretly introduce destructive heresies, even denying the Master who bought them, bringing swift destruction upon themselves.
2 Many will follow their sensuality, and because of them the way of the truth will be maligned;
3 and in their greed they will exploit you with false words; their judgment from long ago is not idle,

and their destruction is not asleep.

2Peter 2:1-3 (NASB)

Making a living, preaching the word of God, isn't wrong. Check this out …

9 For it is written in the Law of Moses, "You shall not muzzle the ox while he is threshing." God is not concerned about oxen, is He? 10 Or is He speaking altogether for our sake? Yes, for our sake it was written, because the plowman ought to plow in hope, and the thresher to thresh in hope of sharing the crops. 11 If we sowed spiritual things in you, is it too much if we reap material things from you? 12 If others share the right over you, do we not more? Nevertheless, we did not use this right, but we endure all things so that we will cause no hindrance to the gospel of Christ. 13 Do you not know that those who perform sacred services eat the food of the temple, and those who attend regularly to the altar have their share from the altar? 14 So also the Lord directed those who proclaim the gospel to get their living from the gospel.

1Corinthians 9:9-14 (NASB)

What is wrong is greedy religious hucksters who con poor dullards into giving them their hard-earned cash so that they can buy either a Lambo or a pagoda.

Finally, the main reason Jesus raged against false prophets and exposed them in pretty much every chapter in the book of Matthew is this: They send people to hell whom Jesus came to redeem and thus He embraced the masculine task of confronting such liars.

Chapter 33

Hole Diggers Or Risk Takers? Matthew 25:14-30

---

14 "For it is just like a man about to go on a journey,
who called his own slaves and entrusted his possessions
to them. 15 To one he gave five talents, to another, two,
and to another, one, each according to his own ability;
and he went on his journey. 16 Immediately the one who
had received the five talents went and traded with them,
and gained five more talents. 17 In the same manner the
one who had received the two talents gained two more.
18 But he who received the one talent went away, and
dug a hole in the ground and hid his master's money.

19 "Now after a long time the master of those slaves
came and settled accounts with them. 20 The one who
had received the five talents came up and brought five
more talents, saying, 'Master, you entrusted five talents
to me. See, I have gained five more talents.' 21 His mas-
ter said to him, 'Well done, good and faithful slave. You
were faithful with a few things, I will put you in charge
of many things; enter into the joy of your master.'

22 "Also the one who had received the two talents
came up and said, 'Master, you entrusted two talents to
me. See, I have gained two more talents.' 23 His master
said to him, 'Well done, good and faithful slave. You
were faithful with a few things, I will put you in charge
of many things; enter into the joy of your master.'

24 "And the one also who had received the one talent
came up and said, 'Master, I knew you to be a hard
man, reaping where you did not sow and gathering
where you scattered no seed. 25 And I was afraid, and
went away and hid your talent in the ground. See, you
have what is yours.'

26 "But his master answered and said to him, 'You
wicked, lazy slave, you knew that I reap where I did
not sow and gather where I scattered no seed. 27 Then
you ought to have put my money in the bank, and on my
arrival I would have received my money back with in-
terest. 28 Therefore take away the talent from him, and
give it to the one who has the ten talents.'

29 "For to everyone who has, more shall be given, and
he will have an abundance; but from the one who does
not have, even what he does have shall be taken away.
30 Throw out the worthless slave into the outer dark-
ness; in that place there will be weeping and gnashing
of teeth.

Matthew 25:14-30 (NASB)

This tale from the Master's mouth starts off rather chipper. The Master calls in three dudes who are his slaves. That means they've got no cash and no condo in Las Olas, Florida.

In addition, they have no vision, no dream and no five year plan which means … horror of horrors … their Instagram page sucks.

There are zero prospects for them until … boom … the Master gifts them with the opportunity of a lifetime! A truckload of cash was given to each one. Some experts say that a 'talent' was worth about two million U.S. dollars.

Check it out: these dudes went from being like Kunte Kinte to kickin' it like Kanye, all in one sweet day.

So this story starts off with grace. The slaves didn't deserve, earn or work for what they got. Neither did they initiate this transaction. It was all the Master's doing. They were just the recipients of this great gift of which two of them doubled and the other one buried. Which leads me to this question: What have we done with what we've been given by God?

We know what the slaves in this story were given, but what have we been given?

I'd say, especially as Americans, that we have been given a ton just by being in the United States of America.

For whiners, or entitlement droogies, who're having a hard time fleshing out a list of what you've been given, please allow me to assist you.

Howzabout this for starters?

First off, I'm guessing that if you're reading this book that you're alive and the Coronavirus didn't kill you off and you have your health. Sure you're living in mommy's basement and you're 30+ years old and it's pretty shameful but at least you're not dead which means you can change that haggard thing you call a life.

Secondly, I'm going to go out on a limb here and conclude that you have a few natural talents, loves, interests, some cash and a little brainpower ... I hope.

Thirdly, if you're a true Christian, then your past, present and future sins are forgiven. Jesus Christ, who is King of Kings and Lord of Lords, is your Lord and Savior. The same Spirit that raised Christ from the dead now dwells in you and because of Jesus' sacrifice for your sins you can now come boldly to the throne of grace and receive help in the time of need from The Omnipotent Triune Godhead who's open 24/7/365.

Now that we know our natural life and our supernatural Lord have given us many useful and dynamic things to use, the question now becomes, 'What the heck have I been doing with what I have been given?'

Here's something to put on your refrigerator: 'Whatever the Lord gives you now, He will ask you about later.' Anyway ...

Where were we?

So the master gives his servants all of his cash. Please note that he didn't tell them what to do with the money. He left that entirely up to them.

I'm sure some are thinking, 'Oh Yeah? So what's your point?' Well, my point is this: God wants us to dream, dare, risk, think, create and exercise initiative as image-bearers of a very Creative God. Yep, God wants us to dream about how best to utilize the treasures He's granted us for Him and His kingdom.

Jesus said the first servant moved out immediately and got busy with his fresh five talents. No grass growing under that bro's feet.

No, 'I want to be sure it's safe' nonsense. He jumps at the opportunity.

The second servant does the same thing. He, too, got creative and busy.

Which brings us to the third servant.

What did old numbnuts do or rather, not do?

When he went to bed that night, his mind was not racing. This dude's not dreaming about great things. He's thinking, 'what part of the backyard can me, the non-adventurous chicken, hide my gift?'

Here's a scary thought: From that day, until the day the Master returned, that Sleestak's life wasn't one iota different. The amazing gift didn't spawn any dreams or any risks. It didn't change him at all.

Churches often talk about the sins of commissions. Y'know … like don't guzzle Gin, don't bang a hooker, don't smoke cigarettes, or become like Nancy Pelosi. They focus on what *not* to do.

Scripture paints equally heinous the sins of omission, i.e. the stuff that you should've done but you didn't and that's the sin of the third slave.

Indeed, the sin of this third servant is not what he did, it's what he didn't do. He didn't make his life an epic adventure of faithfulness to this incredible God.

Every morning he woke up he decided to just sit on this incredible pot of gold his loving Master gave him and do nothing. His life sucked. He was boring.

The other two bros were never going back to normal after the Master interrupted their life with such an explosive gift of grace and Jesus called those two risk takers, 'good and faithful servants.'

Now, you may never have heard this before at your hipster dandy skinny jeans church but being 'good' and 'faithful' is not biblically defined by the Son of Man as maintaining status quo but increasing what's been given one.

The two good servants were like, 'You gave me five talents. I got 10. You gave me two talents. I got four. I multiplied what you gave me. Boom!' They didn't give their Master back the same amount. They multiplied it. And that's the only two he called 'good and faithful servants.'

Check this out all you fear-laden, self-righteous, and smarmy church people.

The third servant didn't lose the Master's money. He didn't gamble it away in Vegas. He didn't get drunk. He didn't commit adultery. He didn't smoke meth. He didn't watch porn or vote for Hillary. You know what else he didn't do? He didn't do anything with the gift the Master gave him and the Master called him 'wicked, slothful and unproductive'.

This third servant had a problem but it wasn't greed, it was fear. He was afraid the Master was a hard man. He was afraid to take a risk. He was afraid he might fail. Garsh … What will people say?

This parable is often taught as a story about stewardship but it's not mostly about stewardship, it's about risk. This dude was terrified to take a risk.

We think our sweet little American Jesus wants us all comfy and risk averse when the exact opposite is true.

Following the true Jesus, the masculine man from Galilee, is a wild ride with no safe spaces, you big wuss. Whoever told you that there would be no risk, no trouble and nothing but non-stop lollipops lied to your dumb backside.

So, get out there and dream.

Get out there and create.

Get out and there build upon and double what The Master has graciously given you.

If we don't, we might hear this from The Master when we take the big dirt nap …

'Throw out the worthless slave into the outer darkness; in that place there will be weeping and gnashing of teeth.'

(* The above was my rough paraphrase of a Rick Godwin sermon)

Chapter 34

Abandoned
Matthew 26:1-4; 55-56

---

1 When Jesus had finished all these words, He said
to His disciples, 2 "You know that after two days the
Passover is coming, and the Son of Man is to be handed
over for crucifixion." 3 Then the chief priests and the
elders of the people were gathered together in the court
of the high priest, named Caiaphas; 4 and they plotted
together to seize Jesus by stealth and kill Him.

55 At that time Jesus said to the crowds, "Have you
come out with swords and clubs to arrest Me as you
would against a robber? Every day I used to sit in
the temple teaching and you did not seize Me. 56 But
all this has taken place to fulfill the Scriptures of the
prophets." Then all the disciples left Him and fled.

Matthew 26:1-4; 55-56 (NASB)

Matthew 26 is one hectic chapter.

Within this chapter the plot to kill Jesus intensifies.

Judas formally commenced his bargaining for Jesus' head with the demonic chief priests whom, I'm-a-guessin', one and all, really regretted that decision now as they slowly roast in Dante's Easy Bake Oven.

In Matthew 26 Jesus confronts the little weasel Judas during dinner and then institutes The Lord's Supper and The New Covenant.

After that momentous occasion, Jesus heads off to The Garden of Gethsemane to pray and fetch strength from the Father for the gruesome death He was about to endure for us chuckleheads. Not only was Jesus about to experience cruel beatings and death but the wrath of God was going to be poured out on Him for our sins.

From that blood sweating prayer time in the Garden of Gethsemane, Jesus gets formally arrested and grilled by that twit, Caiaphas after which the Son of God gets spit on and beat up.

It's times like these you need friends, eh?

No doubt, some GenXers and Boomers, if we were in Jesus' shoes, we would be singing out, or screaming out, this 1965 tune from the Beatles to our closest *compadres* …

"(Help!) I need somebody
(Help!) Not just anybody

(Help!) You know I need someone
(Help!)
Help me if you can, I'm feeling down
And I do appreciate you being 'round
Help me get my feet back on the ground
Won't you please, please help me?"

That's a lot of garbage for one man, even the Son of Man, to field.

We're constantly told to not go through hard times alone and we should lean on close family and friends. That all sounds good and stuff but sometimes your friends suck and you're family is nowhere to be found so … what do you do?

Please note: in Matthew 26 Jesus' handpicked disciples, whom He considered friends (John 15:15), did the following to Him in His greatest hour of need …

1. All twelve of His buddies said they'd never deny Him and that they'd die for Him (Matthew 26:35) and guess what? They denied Him and ran out of there like a chicken with it's head cut off (Matthew 26:56).

2. Judas betrayed Him to His killers for thirty stinkin' pieces of silver. Oh, and by the way, Judas wasn't some ancillary devil. He was one of The Twelve.

3. When Jesus needed some prayer assistance He cried out for help from His bros three times who were fast asleep and drooling on the ground during the greatest event in world history. Yep, they were napping.

4. Peter, the disciple with the foot-shaped mouth, cussed a blue cloud of denial when queried about

being one of Christ's closest confidants. So much for that Michael W. Smith song about 'Friends', eh?

5. Oh, I nearly forgot. Where was the Virgin Mary during all of this?

Jesus, on the night prior to his death, when He's being abandoned, wrongly accused and set up for execution, doesn't call the suicide hotline.

He doesn't start yelling, 'I want my mama!'

Instead, he has his last meal with his boys and then goes off to pray that God'll give him strength to receive the substitutionary death penalty placed upon his sinless, sacrificial body for our shady ways. And that, my friends, is something no man I know would ever do.

Also, when Jesus went to jail and he didn't squeal about it. Oh, and by the way, they abused him in prison and yet he didn't cry, freak or scream. That's dude stuff.

Jesus lost all of his friends. They all fled. There were no Facebook friends to throw Him a life-line. Poof. They're all gone and He still plowed on and did what he had to do even though it was the most difficult thing any human being has ever done.

When talking about Jesus' masculinity one has to stand back and be gobsmacked how He rocked through this intense time just in Matthew 26 all alone.

Think about it: the sins of the whole world were about to be shouldered by Him, together with a humiliating trial and vicious beatings culminating in a hellish execution and He had none of His buddies to back Him for moral support.

He only had the Father.

Which meant that Jesus had everyone He needed, in the Father, to ford through every demon in hell and bridle His reluctant flesh.

Sometimes folks, you've got to go at it alone.

And yes, your friends and family will let you down like you will let them down but the Christian will be okay because, 'The Lord is my shepherd, I shall not want' (Psalm 23:1).

Can I get an, 'Amen'?

Chapter 35

Crucify Him!
Matthew 27:19-23

---

*19 While he was sitting on the judgment seat, his wife sent him a message, saying, "Have nothing to do with that righteous Man; for last night I suffered greatly in a dream because of Him." 20 But the chief priests and the elders persuaded the crowds to ask for Barabbas and to put Jesus to death. 21 But the governor said to them, "Which of the two do you want me to release for you?" And they said, "Barabbas." 22 Pilate said to them, "Then what shall I do with Jesus who is called Christ?" They all *said, "Crucify Him!" 23 And he said, "Why, what evil has He done?" But they kept shouting all the more, saying, "Crucify Him!"*

Matthew 27:19-23 (NASB)

Don't you just love self-righteous religious people?

Yep, if you don't tow their line of stupid works-based salvation blather then they will have you killed.

At least that's what they did back in Jesus' day.

In our day they stop following you on social media and write bitter screeds about you on their unread blogs.

Whether it's with words, swords, or crosses you can bet your backside if someone is getting executed, persecuted, or slandered there's a self-righteous religious jackass at the front of that hate-line stoking on the scorn.

Jesus, throughout His three year earthly ministry, received verbal wrath from the religious rapscallions He roasted.

Now, it was going to get physical.

As in, very physical.

But Jesus was ready.

He'd prayed through to His Father in the Garden of Gethsemane and had fetched the mighty power of The Holy Ghost which made Him act a man (1Corinthians 16:13) in the face of a rogue trial, disgusting mockings and a ghastly crucifixion.

In Matthew 27, Jesus stood before the governor who could've let him go but Jesus held His ground, stuck to what He knew to be true; which led to a beating that no macho-man on Instagram could stand for ten seconds.

After Jesus was beat to a pulp He was crucified.

It's weird when you Google paintings of Christ's crucifixion because there is no blood. Or very little blood. And yet, it was the most gory form of torture and murder one can imagine.

I did a rendition of Christ on the cross in my Biblical Badass Series that you can see by logging on to DougGiles.Art. I made certain the Jesus I depicted was a bloody mess because I always wanted me, the owner of the original painting, those who purchase prints of it and those who simply view it online to forever remember He was shredded for our transgressions.

Matter of fact, here's a medical description of the crucifixion of Jesus Christ.

> The physical trauma of Christ begins in Gethsemane with one of the initial aspects of His suffering - the bloody sweat. Under great emotional stress, tiny capillaries in the sweat glands can break, thus mixing blood with sweat. This process alone could have produced marked weakness and possible shock.
>
> After the arrest in the middle of the night, Jesus was brought before the Sanhedrin. A soldier struck Jesus across the face for remaining silent when questioned by Caiaphas. The palace guards blindfolded Him and mockingly taunted Him as they each passed by and spat on Him and struck Him in the face.
>
> In the early morning, Jesus, battered and bruised, is taken to Jerusalem. It was there that Pilate ordered Jesus scourging and crucifixion.
>
> Preparations for the scourging are carried out. The prisoner is stripped of His clothing and His hands tied to a post. The Roman legionnaire prepares to beat Him with a short-whip consisting of several heavy leaded leather thongs.
>
> At first the heavy thongs cut through the skin only. Then, as the blows continue, they cut deeper into subcutaneous

tissues, producing first an oozing of blood from the capillaries and veins of the skin, and finally spurting arterial bleeding from vessels in the underlying muscles. Finally the skin of the back is hanging in long ribbons and the entire area is an unrecognizable mass of bleeding tissue. When it is determined that the prisoner is near death, the beating is stopped.

Jesus is then untied and allowed to slump to the stone pavement, wet with His own blood. The soldiers see a great joke in this Jew claiming to be a king. They throw a robe across His shoulders and place a stick in His hand for a scepter. A crown of thorns is pressed into His scalp.

After mocking Him and striking Him across the face, the soldiers take the stick from His hand and drive the thorns deeper into His scalp. Finally, they tire of their sadism and the robe is torn from his back. This had already become adherent to the wounds, and its removal, was as though He were again being whipped.

The heavy beam of the cross is then tied across His shoulders, and the procession begins its slow journey, to Golgotha. The weight of the heavy wooden beam, together with the shock produced by blood loss, is too much. He stumbles and falls.

At Golgotha, the beam is placed on the ground and Jesus is quickly thrown backward with His shoulders against the wood. The beam is then lifted in place at the top of the posts and the titulus reading, "Jesus of Nazareth, King of the Jews" is nailed in place.

Now nailed to the cross, Christ's arms fatigue, great waves of cramps sweep over the muscles, knotting them in deep, relentless, throbbing pain. With these cramps comes the inability to push Himself upward.

Hanging by His arms, the pectoral muscles are unable to act. Air can be drawn into the lungs, but cannot be exhaled. Finally, carbon dioxide builds up in the lungs and in the bloodstream and the cramps partially subside. Spas-

> modically, He is able to push Himself upward to exhale and bring in the life-giving oxyGenesis
>
> After hours of agonizing pain another agony begins. A deep crushing pain deep in the chest as the pericardium slowly fills with serum and begins to compress the heart.
>
> He can feel the chill of death creeping through His tissues. With one last surge of strength, He once again presses His torn feet against the nail, straightens His legs, takes a deeper breath, and utters His seventh and last cry, "Father, into thy hands I commit my spirit."
>
> Apparently to make doubly sure of death, the legionnaire drove his lance through the fifth inner space between the ribs, upward through the pericardium and into the heart. Immediately there came out blood and water. We, therefore, have rather conclusive postmortem evidence that our Lord died, not the usual crucifixion death by suffocation, but of heart failure due to shock and constriction of the heart by fluid in the pericardium.

(* Condensed from "The Crucifixion of Jesus"
by C. Truman Davis, M.S.)

As brutal as the physical pain must've been, the pain of having the Father, for a moment, forsake Him as Jesus took the Father's wrath out on Him instead of us sinners is, to me, unimaginable.

Nevertheless, The Man, Christ Jesus, endured the cross, despised the shame and is now seated at the right hand of the Father. His sinless life and His brutal and bloody sacrificial death satisfied the holiness and righteousness of God and now anyone (good, bad or ugly) who believes is saved through Jesus' finished work and there isn't one little goody-two-shoe-religious work you can do to add to what He has done.

Paul put it this way …

20 Therefore, we are ambassadors for Christ, as though God were making an appeal through us; we beg you on behalf of Christ, be reconciled to God. 21 He made Him who knew no sin to be sin on our behalf, so that we might become the righteousness of God in Him.

2Corinthians 5:20,21 (NASB)

Isaiah put it this way …

Who has believed our message?

And to whom has the arm of the Lord been revealed?

2 For He grew up before Him like a tender shoot,

And like a root out of parched ground;

He has no stately form or majesty

That we should look upon Him,

Nor appearance that we should be attracted to Him.

3 He was despised and forsaken of men,

A man of sorrows and acquainted with grief;

And like one from whom men hide their face

He was despised, and we did not esteem Him.

4 Surely our griefs He Himself bore,

And our sorrows He carried;

Yet we ourselves esteemed Him stricken,

Smitten of God, and afflicted.

5 But He was pierced through for our transgressions,

He was crushed for our iniquities;

The chastening for our well-being fell upon Him,

And by His scourging we are healed.

6 All of us like sheep have gone astray,

Each of us has turned to his own way;

But the Lord has caused the iniquity of us all

To fall on Him.

7 He was oppressed and He was afflicted,

Yet He did not open His mouth;

Like a lamb that is led to slaughter,

And like a sheep that is silent before its shearers,

So He did not open His mouth.

8 By oppression and judgment He was taken away;

And as for His generation, who considered

That He was cut off out of the land of the living

For the transgression of my people, to whom the stroke was due?

9 His grave was assigned with wicked men,

Yet He was with a rich man in His death,

Because He had done no violence,

Nor was there any deceit in His mouth.

10 But the Lord was pleased

To crush Him, putting Him to grief;

If He would render Himself as a guilt offering,

He will see His offspring,

He will prolong His days,

And the good pleasure of the Lord will prosper in His hand.

11 As a result of the anguish of His soul,

He will see it and be satisfied;

By His knowledge the Righteous One,

My Servant, will justify the many,

As He will bear their iniquities.

12 Therefore, I will allot Him a portion with the great,

And He will divide the booty with the strong;

Because He poured out Himself to death,

And was numbered with the transgressors;

Yet He Himself bore the sin of many,

And interceded for the transgressors.

Isaiah 53 (NASB)

Chapter 36

WWJD, Indeed
Matthew 28:16-18

---

19 While he was sitting on the judgment seat, his wife
sent him a message, saying, "Have nothing to do with
that righteous Man; for last night I suffered greatly in
a dream because of Him." 20 But the chief priests and
the elders persuaded the crowds to ask for Barabbas
and to put Jesus to death. 21 But the governor said to
them, "Which of the two do you want me to release for
*you?" And they said, "Barabbas." 22 Pilate *said to*
them, "Then what shall I do with Jesus who is called
*Christ?" They all *said, "Crucify Him!" 23 And he*
said, "Why, what evil has He done?" But they kept
shouting all the more, saying, "Crucify Him!"

Matthew 27:19-23 (NASB)

Question: If you just had the shiitake mushrooms beat out of you and then you were executed and left to morph into worm dirt in a dank cave and then, supernaturally, boom, you sprang back to life after being three days gone … what would you do?

Most Christians nowadays would take several selfies in front of the tomb, hanging out with the angel and then load those pics on the 'gram, PDQ.

Some Christians would blog about their amazing experience, hire an agent and try to get on Oprah to pimp their new book, *Three Days In A Hole: How I Turned A Negative Into A Positive.*

Others would take a long vacation and try to recover from the emotional, spiritual, and physical trauma they just experienced. Of course, such a holiday would entail many spa days and a mani and pedi for the hipster males that just went through some very trying times.

So, what was one of the first things that Jesus did, according to Matthew's account, after being beaten and murdered and stuck in a cave to rot for three long days?

What would Jesus do?

Well, you inquiring mind, Jesus went mountain climbing.

Yep, Him and His posse headed to the hills.

I know some genteel Christians who can't climb mountains because they're too frail from being a tinkerpot too long.

I know other Christians who can't climb mountains because they're addicted to chicken fried steak.

But Jesus, fresh from defeating death, hell and the grave,

headed for the hills for His reunion with His boys.

Indeed, they didn't go to Starbucks, the mall, or an AOC rally, or to some rescue animal shelter. They went to the mountains.

But it wasn't for some little kumbaya meeting.

Oh, heck no.

Jesus was all business and went straight into commissioning these former rough cussing fishermen into the heralds of the Gospel who were to baptize and teach nations all that He had commanded them. That's what you call, 'Dude stuff.'

And that's a wrap, folks.

If I haven't convinced you, heretofore, through the weight of the scripture, that Jesus was decisively masculine, and that was and is a good thing, then I don't have the time, patience, or crayons to further explain it to you.

Chapter 37

How Would Jesus Riot? Matthew 21:12-13

*12 And Jesus entered the temple and drove out all those who were buying and selling in the temple, and overturned the tables of the money changers and the seats of those who were selling doves. 13 And He *said to them, "It is written, 'My house shall be called a house of prayer'; but you are making it a robbers' den."*

Matthew 21:12,13 (NASB)

Jesus was not above kicking some butt and breaking stuff if need be. Look, Jesus was no wussy. For example, one of the first snapshots we have of Jesus in John's account of his ministry was his turning water into wine and cleansing the temple, two things the teetotalers and the timid do not like being in the sacred text.

Check it out in John 2:13-17 (NASB):

> *13 The Passover of the Jews was near, and Jesus went*
> *up to Jerusalem. 14 And He found in the temple those*
> *who were selling oxen and sheep and doves, and the*
> *money changers seated at their tables. 15 And He made*
> *a scourge of cords, and drove them all out of the tem-*
> *ple, with the sheep and the oxen; and He poured out*
> *the coins of the money changers and overturned their*
> *tables; 16 and to those who were selling the doves He*
> *said, "Take these things away; stop making My Fa-*
> *ther's house a place of business." 17 His disciples re-*
> *membered that it was written, "Zeal for Your house will*
> *consume me."*

Let's break Matthew and John's snapshot of Christ crashing the temple, shall we? I think it's very important that we understand how to follow Jesus's example, in all things, especially in regard to protesting and righting egregious wrongs.

First off, please take note of the offense that got Jesus in a bad mood: Religious hucksters had turned God's house into a cash cow for snake oil salesmen. In other words, it was a clear-cut, irrefutable offense, with empirical evidence, that got Christ's dander up. Ponder that nugget before you burn down an innocent couple's grocery store, *por favor*.

This led, as stated, to Jesus' going postal on the place. But what I'd like to point out was how Jesus released his rage as an example to us schleps that follow his lead, if and when it comes to dusting up against some true injustice. Are you ready? Well, alrighty then.

Herewith are the various particulars regarding how the

Holy One rolled.

1. Jesus made a whip, which screams to me, that he was patient and methodical and it wasn't belligerent, out of control, frenzied rage he sported.

2. Jesus only vandalized the evil SOBs' stuff that were desecrating God's house. Please note, he didn't morph into a crazy vandal.

3. Jesus didn't steal their stuff after condemning their actions. Hello!

4. Jesus had a clear biblical mandate that God's house was to be a house of prayer and that zeal for its purity drove his legit wrath.

5. Jesus didn't cleanse the temple incognito. He wasn't anonymous. He wore no weird mask, or a bandana over his face, or a hoodie and shades. People who do that are nutless wonders. If you're so bold and so in the right, then like Jesus, represent … stand up and be counted.

6. Jesus didn't make a living off grievance-based temple-tossing. He didn't form a non-profit that went around making life miserable for everyone he thought sucked. Also, he acted alone, without some massive posse and there are only two examples of him ever engaging in such acts.

7. Jesus never said to his disciples, "lets burn this bitch down". Please note, he also didn't call them "motherf***kers" as his wrath was bridled.

And that, my little children, is how Christ threw a holy fit. Anything else is … well … uh … un-Christlike and must be repented of and condemned.

Finally, for the slow amongst us who claim Christ as their captain please note in Jesus's example of opening up a can of whup-ass that …

- There was no stealing.
- There was no arson.
- There was no stoking of a phony revolt based on lies. Empirical evidence drove Jesus' cleansing of the temple.
- There was no unnecessary destruction of property.
- There were no incitements to riots.
- He didn't threaten to rape and/or murder his enemies' women and kids.
- And he wasn't impulsive in his anger and reduced to animalistic destruction.

Jesus was an example of how to deal with egregious wrongs without losing one's head.

Chapter 38

Please God, Don't Make Me Be A Christian

"The effeminate ... will not inherit the Kingdom of God..."

-1Corinthians 6:9
(Doug Giles Translation)

Here's my personal testimony. I didn't go to a church until I got converted at the age of twenty-one. My parents weren't drug dealers or sex traffickers, they just didn't claim to be Christians, so they didn't pretend to be by going to church. And you know what? I appreciate that.

Yep, we didn't go to church at all. Not on Easter or Christmas. I'm talking about no immediate church experience for me. Not even weddings or funerals. Indeed, there were zero kumbaya gatherings for this Cretin.

What I knew about Christians was primarily via the guys and gals I bumped up against in high school.

What I gained from my interactions with the Christian males I ran into was this: They're self righteous softies who wanted me to go to hell. Suffice it to say, we didn't get along at all and becoming a Christian was not on my 'To Do List'.

But God had other plans …

From the age of thirteen to twenty-one I was hell on two skinny legs. I started drinking pretty heavily and regularly at thirteen and around sixteen I saw *Fast Times At Ridgemont Hig*h and started taking notes. By the end of that year I was dealing weed, LSD and speed.

I was an evil little monster. I was not a good person. Not at all.

All I wanted was sex, a solid buzz, a fast car and that was it. I kept it simple, because I was stupid.

Please note: I was not on a spiritual quest. I did not want to be a Christian and I heartily expected that if I died my elevator would not be going up. I was going straight to hell. I was under no delusions about 'being a good boy, who meant well, but was troubled.' I knew I was damned and honestly, I was okay with that … for a while.

I won't bore you with the details, but God had my number and I started feeling 'weird' when I would do bad crap beginning around the age of eighteen and, heretofore, I had never felt bad. It was all a big joke to me.

Around 1981 that callousness began to erode.

At that stage of the game, I was way down the funnel of evil and it wasn't funny anymore and people were being hurt and I was getting arrested.

The stakes were high and so was I.

I knew I needed a change but I did not want to start going to church because most of the Christian males I met in high school were wussies and I didn't not want to be a wussy.

So, instead of becoming a choir boy, I started dialing back on my partying and started working out. 'Exercise versus excess', I thought. That was my solution to my current level of pollution which wasn't totally bad, mind you.

It was however, short lived. My conscience was still kicking my butt. The working out wasn't drowning out the guilt I had for what I had done and who I knew I was at my core namely, a sinner. *Ergo*, I did what any good sinner would do and cranked back up the drinking, sex, and drug machine to silence 'the voices.'

My next three years were really bad. I don't even remember most of them. Just lots of booze, weed, acid, and cocaine.

I'll never forget one night me and my buddy Joe were cooking on some blotter, hanging out at a closed public pool, just tripping away and talking about … God?

Yep, we were talking about God. Wondering if He existed and if there was a right and wrong and how, if there was the aforementioned, and we had to meet Him, then man oh, man; were we on the wrong side of that equation. But still, nothing of substance changed in me.

It was at that juncture, when I was finally entertaining God, righteousness, death, and judgment that I started getting bombarded with thoughts from my evil angels saying, 'You don't want to be a Christian. Christians are wussies. People will mock you. Who wants to be that?' And like an idiot, I believed that low-level devil and I carried on in my self-destructive course, blowing off God and indulging deeply in what Saint Peter called, 'the superfluity of naughtiness'. That was until December 7th, 1983. On that fateful night God poleaxed me.

Here's how it went down.

My dad and I were watching NBC Nightly News with Tom Brokaw and Tom was talking about a fourteen-year-old kid who'd just graduated college. I was twenty-one-years old and had just been kicked out of college and Brokaw's little vignette on this over-achiever made me feel like Beavis & Butthead on steroids. I felt like I should've felt: like a loser. My dad didn't say a word but I knew what he was thinking namely, 'when is he going to get his act together?'

Following my normal course of action after getting convicted of my sin, I went and got my girlfriend at Texas Tech, my weed stash, and a 12-pack of Silver Bullets and off we went to get high and bump uglies.

While we were partying in my car, out of nowhere, I told my main squeeze that I wanted to go home. She's like, 'We just got here. What's wrong?' I said, nothing and that I just want to go home. She said ok and off we went, back home in the middle of our 'date.'

When I got back to my house my girlfriend and I got into an argument that got pretty heated out in front of my house. It was so loud that my dad and brother came outside to see what the heck was going on. When my dad stepped off the porch and started heading towards me in the driveway I ran towards him, embraced him and asked him to forgive me for all the horrible crap I'd done to him and mom. I collapsed. I wept. Everyone was like, 'Whiskey. Tango. Foxtrot!' Where did this come from? I was broken. I was shattered. The game was over.

After I'd calmed down a bit, my girlfriend and I loaded back up in my car and off we went to drop her off at her dorm. However, we didn't get very far. It started hitting me again. Namely, a massive sense of guilt and conviction. It was so bad that I had to pull my vehicle over in an apartment parking lot. My girl's really freaking now. 'What's wrong? What's happening to you?' she asked. All I could do was weep. And I mean capital W-E-E-P, weep. Finally, out from under the massive flow of tears and phlegm, I said to God, not to her, 'God if you're real and if Jesus is who people say he is then please change me.' And boom. It happened.

On December 7th, 1983, I got converted and it was radical and ugly. Immediately I stopped the drugs and the booze abuse. I no longer wanted it. I wanted God instead. My former vices no longer appealed to me. All I wanted to do was pursue the God who pursued me, the clod.

Now, in case you missed it, let me reiterate what was a major sticking point to my aversion to becoming a Christian. It was something that the powers of darkness really used against me, the rebel without a clue. It was this; if I became a Christian, based on what I saw and heard from Christians in high school, that means that I would have to become a wussy and becoming a wussy appeared nowhere on my Christmas wish list.

For example: I experienced major, and I mean major conviction, and yet I didn't want to become a Christian because of the effeminized Christian males I'd met. I was almost bargaining with God. It went something like this, 'Please forgive me, let me go to heaven, but don't make me sing sappy songs, wear nerdy 'Christian' clothes and act like Jim Bakker on The PTL Club, or like that lame dork named, Todd, the Youth Group director.

I kid you not.

I wanted to be forgiven but I did not want to become a 'Christian'.

Again, from what I'd gathered from interacting with male, high school Christians, was that Jesus and church attendance gelds a guy and gelded I did not want to get.

These were real problems to me as a young turk who'd grown up watching the likes of Clint Eastwood, John Wayne, Steve McQueen, The Dallas Cowboys, and being around WWII adults.

Yes, my lofty aspirations, when I actually had some, were to kill dragons, save nations, and throttle some enemy with a Raquel Welch clone at my side. Wearing a cardigan, singing *I'll Fly Away*, while holding hands with other men, as we talk about our feelings and how wrong it is to masturbate was nightmarish to me.

It was not cool.

It was not inspiring.

It was not masculine.

And I wanted, more than anything, as a lost man, to be masculine. As all boys do. Aside from Bruce Jenner, of course. But my sins had become too much for me to bear and I caved. God won. I got converted and a couple of months later I finally went to church. And you know what? All my suspicions were spot on. It was very effeminate.

Mind you, and pardon my redundancy, I had no knowledge base about what went down in church having never, ever, been before. I just knew what I knew about believers from high school and seeing the scary peeps on The PTL Club at my aunt's house when we would visit. I came in raw and I'll never forget my first blush with the brethren. Never. All my fears were spot on. The Church, by and large, had been severely effeminized.

Thank God I met some bro's who loved God and didn't like to knit but liked to hunt and fish instead. I also met some epic dudes who loved God wholeheartedly and liked to debate and do jail, street, bar, and rock concert ministry and radical missions way down deep in Mexican jungles.

Look folks, God hardwired men, in His image, to be providers, protectors, hunters, and heroes under His governance. For pastors or anyone else to try to effeminize the *Imago Dei* and foist that lie upon men's psyche, is to bastardize the scripture, deceive men into denying their God-given masculine traits and to me, that ranks up there with the Unpardonable Sin.

About The Author.

Doug earned his Bachelor of Fine Arts degree from Texas Tech University and his certificates in both Theological and Biblical Studies from Knox Theological Seminary (Dr. D. James Kennedy, Chancellor). Giles was fortunate to have Dr. R.C. Sproul as an instructor for many classes.

Doug Giles is the co-founder and co-host of the *Warriors & Wildmen* podcast (500K downloads) and the man behind ClashDaily.com. In addition to driving ClashDaily.com (250M+ page views), Giles is the author of several #1 Amazon bestsellers including, *Rules For Radical Christians: 10 Biblical Disciplines of Influential Believers*.

Doug is also an artist and a filmmaker and his online gallery can be seen at DougGiles.Art. His first film, *Biblical Badasses: A Raw Look At Christianity and Art*, is available via Amazon Prime Video.

Doug's writings have appeared on several other print and online news sources, including Townhall.com, The Washington Times, The Daily Caller, Fox Nation, Human Events, USA Today, The Wall Street Journal, The Washington Examiner, American Hunter Magazine, and ABC News.

Giles and his wife Margaret have two daughters, Hannah and Regis. Hannah devastated ACORN with her 2009 nation-shaking undercover videos and she currently stars in the explosive, 2018 Tribeca Documentary, Acorn and The Firestorm. Regis has been featured in Elle, American Hunter, and Variety magazines. Regis is also the author of a powerful new book titled, How Not To Be A #Me-Too Victim, But A #WarriorChick. Regis and Hannah are both black belts in Gracie/Valente Jiu-Jitsu.

Speaking Engagements

To invite Doug to speak at your next event, log on to DougGiles.org and fill out the invitation request.

Accolades for Giles include …

– Giles was recognized as one of "The 50 Best Conservative Columnists Of 2015"

– Giles was recognized as one of "The 50 Best Conservative Columnists Of 2014"

– Giles was recognized as one of "The 50 Best Conservative Columnists Of 2013"

– ClashDaily.com was recognized as one of "The 100 Most Popular Conservative Websites For 2013 and 2020"

– Doug was noted as "Hot Conservative New Media Superman" By Politichicks

Between 2002 – 2006, Doug's 3-minute daily commentary in Miami received seven Silver Microphone Awards and two Communicator Awards.

What others say about Doug Giles

For a generation, at least, Western Society has been leveling its ideological guns on men -- that is on males, "maleness". For a good chunk of that stretch, Doug Giles -- author, hunter, commentator, broadcaster -- has taken up the cause of his fellow "dudes". His latest salvo in this desperately needed pro-XY chromosome crusade is If Masculinity Is 'Toxic', Call Jesus Radioactive. Delivered in the lively, inimitable style those familiar with Doug have come to recognize, the book confronts modern-day misandry, head on. The significance of dads, husbands, sons, brothers -- men! -- has become one of the gasping and endangered themes of our effeminized, gender-addled era. With the release of this newest tome, Doug aims to pump some life back into that foundational truth. If Masculinity Is 'Toxic', Call Jesus Radioactive tracks through the Gospel of Matthew -- a winning, easy-to-follow format -- highlighting how Jesus demonstrates what God expects of men. For all that, the book goes a long way toward sketching much of what the Creator envisions for every person -- so the ladies will benefit from perusing these pages as well.

Steve Pauwels
Editor-In-Chief, DailySurge.com

"Giles aims his arrows at the pusillanimous pastors who have bred a generation of mamby pamby Christian men who cower before the wicked. Giles challenges 'Rise up O men of God!'"

- Steven Hotze, MD
Hotze Health & Wellness Center

Doug's podcast can be seen and heard at

WarriorsAndWildmen.com.

Books by Doug Giles

Shout At The Devil: The Warrior's Confession Guide (Coming Soon)

Would Jesus Vote For Trump?

Rules For Radical Christians: 10 Biblical Disciplines for Influential Believers

Pussification: The Effeminization Of The American Male

Raising Righteous And Rowdy Girls

Raising Boys Feminists Will Hate

Rise, Kill and Eat: A Theology of Hunting From Genesis to Revelation.

If You're Going Through Hell, Keep Going

My Grandpa is a Patriotic Badass

A Coloring Book for College Cry Babies

Sandy Hook Massacre: When Seconds Count, Police Are Minutes Away

The Bulldog Attitude: Get It or ... Get Left Behind

A Time To Clash

10 Habits of Decidedly Defective People: The Successful Loser's Guide to Life

Political Twerps, Cultural Jerks, Church Quirks

It has been said that daughters are God's revenge on fathers for the kind of men they were when they were young. Some would say that both Doug Giles and I, given our infamous pasts, are charter members of that club. However, Doug and I know that his two wonderful daughters and my equally wonderful daughter and two granddaughters are truly God's fantastic gift. With the wisdom of hindsight and experience Doug has written the ultimate manual for dads on raising righteous and rowdy daughters who will go out into the world well prepared- morally, physically, intellectually and with joyful hearts- to be indomitable and mighty lionesses in our cultural jungle. Through every raucous and no-holds-barred page, Doug, the incomparable Dad Drill Sergeant, puts mere men through the paces to join the ranks of the few, the proud, and the successful fathers of super daughters. The proof of Doug Giles' gold-plated credentials are Hannah and Regis Giles- two of the most fantastic, great hearted and accomplished young ladies I have ever known. This is THE BOOK that I will be giving the father of my two precious five and three year old granddaughters. Tiger Mom meet Lion Dad!

— Pat Caddell

Former Fox News Contributor —

Check out Doug's art
work at DougGiles.Art

Shout At The Devil

Overcoming Fear

Coming Soon!

The Warrior's Confession Guide

Doug Giles

Made in the USA
Coppell, TX
02 July 2020

30041706R00155